THE GLASTONBURY TAROT

THE GLASTONBURY TAROT

WRITTEN AND ILLUSTRATED
BY LISA TENZIN-DOLMA

SAMUEL WEISER, INC.

York Beach, Maine

First published in the United States in 1999 by
Samuel Weiser, Inc.
PO Box 612
York Beach, ME 03910-0612
www.weiserbooks.com

This edition published by arrangement with
Gothic Image Publications,
PO Box 2568, Glastonbury, Somerset BA6 8XR, England.
www.gothicimage.co.uk

Library of Congress Catalog Card Number: 99-63996

ISBN 1-57863-140-8

Printed & bound by C&C Offset Printing Co., Hong Kong

07   06   05   04   03   02   01   00   99
10   9   8   7   6   5   4   3   2   1

THE GLASTONBURY TAROT IS DEDICATED
TO BETTY AND HAROLD.

CONTENTS

ACKNOWLEDGEMENTS 9

FOREWORD by John & Caitlin Matthews 11

INTRODUCTION 15

CHAPTER ONE: Meeting the Tarot 19

CHAPTER TWO: How To Use Your Tarot Cards 23

THE MAJOR ARCANA 33

THE MINOR ARCANA 101

Staffs 103
Chalices 119
Swords 135
Vesicas 153

BIBLIOGRAPHY 167

ACKNOWLEDGEMENTS

Many thanks are due to Frances Howard-Gordon of Gothic Image Publications, who came to me with the idea for the Glastonbury Tarot, and who oversaw it to its conclusion; and to her husband, Jamie George. To John and Caitlin Matthews for writing the Foreword; and to Donald Weiser of Samuel Weiser Publishers, who took on the Rights for the American edition. The vivid oil colours I used for the paintings were very difficult to reproduce - a thousand thanks to Wes for managing it, and for working so tirelessly on the layout with Frances.

Without the wholehearted co-operation of my five children - Ryan, Oliver, Daniel, Liam, and Amber - this work could not have been completed. Big hugs and thanks to them for putting up with erratic mealtimes and a slightly distracted mother while the deadline loomed; and for their constant enthusiasm, feedback, and willingness to model for me. I couldn't wish for a more loving family, and I count my blessings for the gift of their presence in my life. My parents also offered much support, and I thank them.

Several artist friends have inspired me a great deal - Shane Whitehead, Stuart Littlejohn, Trystan Mitchell, Chesca Potter, Jill Smith, Simant Bostock, Willow Roe, Catriona McDonagh, and Andrew Forrest.

This book took 20 months to illustrate and write, and entailed a rather hermit-like existence. To remind me that I wasn't forgotten in that time, many friends came and sat chatting while I painted, made cups of tea and coffee, were lavish in their encouragement, and enthused about being guinea-pigs while I tested the dummy cards out on them. They also thoughtfully stayed away while I wrote the text! Loving thanks to all of them, especially Shane, Vicki, Rebecca, Alison, Maureen, Shirley, Trystan, Joy, Rachel, Helen, Zana, Jo and Chris, Sam and Stuart, Duncan, Fiona, Sangeeta, and Paul L. Thanks to Alison for proof-reading the initial chapters. Also to Sig Lonegren for the Sacred Geometry lesson, and good advice. As for the rest of them, too numerous to mention - you know who you are! Huge thanks also to Duncan for support and friendship, and for looking after the younger children at weekends, and allowing me an undistracted space to work in.

And to the friends who were willing to model for me, I offer large chunks of gratitude. I was in the fortunate (and unusual for an artist) position of having more offers of models than I had tarot cards for! The people I painted were chosen because, to me, they embodied aspects of a particular archetype. I did not use models for the difficult cards because the energy of the tarot image often seemed to manifest in the model's life as well as my own while I worked on it. As six friends who modelled for me became pregnant not long afterwards, it became necessary to issue a 'baby' warning! So to all of my models listed here, many, many thanks: Ryan, Oliver, Daniel, Liam, Amber, Vicki, Ed, Dion, Cathie, Pree, Sam, Stuart, Ian, Frances, Jamie, Rebecca, Shane, Neil, Cheryl, Annie, Dan, Megan, Tracey, Scott, Lisa, Ben, Trystan, Chesca, Mike, Joy, Tanja, Jim, Meli, Justin, Achim, Sue, David, James, Karen, Lez, Simon, Linda, Jo and Chris, Simon and Kristen, Caspar, Chris, Willow, Andrew, Matthew, Be, Steve, Wes, Paula, and Mark.

FOREWORD

Some years ago, the Arthurian scholar, Geoffrey Ashe, (himself a resident of Glastonbury) wrote a wonderful novel called The Finger and the Moon, in which the imagery of the tarot lay hidden, embedded in a story of Avalonian magic, much as the Glastonbury Zodiac underlies and surrounds the town itself. Now Glastonbury has its own tarot in Lisa Tenzin-Dolma's vibrant deck.

There can be very few places in the world that contain sufficient mythic and mystical reference points to furnish 78 cards, but the small market town of Glastonbury is just such a place. The Glastonbury Tarot emerges from the melting pot of ideas, beliefs and wisdom which have been embodied around this extraordinary sacred site for many ages. Indeed, this focus of world-wide pilgrimage has so much mythic energy, that to enter its streets and walk its hills is to become part of the myth.

The tarot is first and foremost about journeys - to work within the imagery of such a pack as the one you hold in your hands, is to enter into a journey of one's own - a life journey that is often seen in terms of a quest. Thus it is particularly appropriate that the major arcana of the Glastonbury Tarot draw upon the imagery of the Arthurian legends - which are themselves built around the transformative quest for the Grail.

To open and use this pack is very like taking a walk through and around Glastonbury itself. In each card there is a sense of wonder which accompanies one at every step, a feeling of entering an otherworldly place where anything can (and frequently does) happen, where a chance meeting around the next corner can presage a whole new direction in one's life. In the minor arcana, the modern pilgrims on this quest and those who live in and around the town, are seen as part of the myth, recipients and mediators of the wisdom. For this is not a quest that only exists in past times: it is an ongoing central feature of many people's spiritual progress today.

Wherever you may be on your own journey, you will find some echo coming back to you from the cards, which are indeed, as the author notes, a mirror held up to every one of us - one that reflects back truth with an accuracy we may scarcely ever have encountered. It is indeed a little bit like standing in the medieval Abbot's Kitchen in the ruins of Glastonbury Abbey, and looking down into the mirror which is so positioned that we can see the roof far above us. The image there is the same yet different - a reflection of the roof, but containing our own image. The tarot does this also - putting our own life and concerns into the pattern of the archetypal world referenced in the cards.

The message of the Glastonbury Tarot to its users is very similar to that which the spirit of Glastonbury whispers to all pilgrims who, like the Fool in this deck, set out in hope for the golden towers of better times and circumstances. Drawing cards from this tarot and using the Bird spread, we offer you this message. It is to find inner equilibrium (Temperance or Brigit) through uncompromisingly facing one's true self (Queen of Swords.) For though we all visit sacred places to find spiritual nurture and a mature, creative way of life (Empress or Guinevere,) our quest is about refreshing our direction, releasing old illusions which ensnare us (8 of Swords) so that we may understand the subtle impressions which are nagging under the surface (7 of Chalices) and to test whether they represent our true vision or not. Many times, we are called to pass "the door without a key" as esotericist, Dion Fortune, (who lived under the shadow of Chalice Hill) called the way into our dreams where we experience true vision (The Moon or Chalice Hill.) When we attend to the information that arises from our quest, we learn that our actions have causation and effect upon our lives and surroundings which causes us to change the way we live (Justice or Arviragus.) This encourages us to re-tune to our vision, and to spend periods of reflection apart in order to receive and welcome the light that ever burns within the soul (The Hermit or St Collen.)

Glastonbury is one among many sacred sites to be visited, but our individual spiritual quest is a pilgrimage that must be consistently pursued in the everyday world. Lisa Tenzin-Dolma's deck opens to us remarkable doors of perception through which we can each access the ancient wisdom of the landscape of Glastonbury, and by inference other and deeper mysteries, at any time we so choose.

John and Caitlin Matthews, June 1999

INTRODUCTION

The tarot is an ancient system of self-knowledge through the use of symbols. The images, in sequence, track a pathway through the journey of the soul - from the trust and innocence of THE FOOL to the wisdom, joy and spiritual liberation of THE WORLD. The cards reveal the tests, trials and triumphs along the way, which we as human beings encounter in our development of the knowledge of who we are.

The tarot cards are divided into two parts. The 22 Major Arcana cards reveal the experiences of life, and the archetypes which bring their energy to those experiences. The 56 Minor Arcana show how we react to those experiences, and how they manifest in our lives. These are divided into a further 4 sections, one for each element: Fire (Staffs), Water (Chalices), Air (Swords), and Earth (Vesicas). Fire relates to action, to inspiration and the use of the will. Water relates to the emotions and the intuitive aspect of ourselves. Air relates to the mind, to the processes of thought and intellect, which can be divisive or unifying. Earth relates to the 'grounding' or manifestation of our energy, and to material considerations.

There are many tarot packs available, so why, you may ask, is this one dedicated to Glastonbury - a tiny town in Somerset, England? The Glastonbury Tarot follows the sequence and symbolism of other traditional tarot cards, but contains within its imagery the inspirational myths, legends, historical figures and sacred sites which abound in this area.

Glastonbury has been known by many names. It is the ancient Isle Of Avalon, the entrance to the Otherworld, a place of magic and mystery. As Ynys Witrin, the Isle Of Glass, this place acts as a mirror, which, when you look into it, shows your soul, your deepest self. Glastonbury has been known as the Isle of the Dead, where secrets are revealed, and as the Isle of Apples, because of its many orchards. It is linked with the Summerland, the beautiful place where souls go to rest.

Since ancient times, when Glastonbury was an island, surrounded by water broken only by lake villages rising from its depths, the area has been richly steeped in history and enigma. Pagan traditions flourished here, co-existing with the first Christian church in the Western Isles, founded by Joseph of Arimathea, the uncle of Jesus. Druids trod their paths through groves and lines of oak trees. Heroes and warriors came here. Saints and seekers of truth journeyed to its shores, and it was long known as "the holiest earthe in England".

As the Isle of Glass, Glastonbury is seen as a mirror which enables seekers to look deep within their hearts, and truly know themselves. It is a place of visions. The light has an unusual, luminous quality which attracts the eye to look deeper, to go within as well as feast itself upon the haunting beauty of the landscape.

Throughout the ages, Glastonbury has been a place set apart - a refuge, the entrance to the Otherworld and the Underworld; a land where time moves different courses, and where realities can shift and merge to birth new and wondrous images and revelations.

In her book, *Glastonbury: Maker Of Myths*, Frances Howard-Gordon observes that living in Glastonbury is like living in a pack of tarot cards. Like the tarot, one is on a journey here. In this unique area are embodied all the archetypes and symbols that are found in the tarot. These are encompassed within the landscape and in the mysticism of earth-lore; in the Arthurian legends, and in Christian history. All paths meet and merge here to form a rich tapestry, the weft and warp of human existence and experience.

Within the Glastonbury Tarot cards is a blending of philosophical paths within the context of the landscape. The illustrations depict the history of the area through Pagan, Christian, and Arthurian figures, reflecting the marriage of belief systems in this small area of land which is a melting-pot of ideas and ideologies, a cauldron of inspiration which feeds all who come here.

Glastonbury breathes spirit through the air which caresses her land. But the energies here also provide an anchor which clarifies and 'grounds' who we are, and what the individual purpose is for our lives. As the magical Isle of Avalon, Glastonbury embodies the place of mystery and beauty that exists within the human heart - no matter where you are geographically. The journey through the Glastonbury Tarot is the journey we all undertake through life, focused and concentrated within this area of land, but relevant everywhere.

In the images depicted in the cards, the landscapes are all of this area. Some are symbolic, others are recognisably rendered. The text for most of the cards will reveal the location of the landscapes, except where I have painted the gardens of friends. Most of the figures in the images are of friends of mine from the area, who I felt embodied aspects of the energies of the cards, and I offer my thanks to them for their inspiration.

The figures in the Major Arcana come from the history, myths and legends associated with Glastonbury. Their stories are told as a prelude to the symbolism and interpretation of the images. This can give you a deeper insight into the meaning of the cards, and also relates some of the rich history and folklore of this area. Each figure has many tales to tell, and an entire book could be written (and in many cases, has been written) about each one. Because of this, I have selected only the stories that bear relevance to each particular image.

The Minor Arcana cards show the landscapes of the area, and marry these in with the symbolism that is reflected in the card.

Before you read the interpretations of the cards, I would recommend that you just sit quietly and observe what each image reveals to you. If you allow the cards to speak to you, you will be able to access the land of deep inner knowing that resides within each of us.

CHAPTER ONE

MEETING THE TAROT

The fundamental function of the tarot cards is to show you reality without judgement. The images reflect the states and experiences you are undergoing, with no sense of 'good' or 'bad'. The cards which show difficulties also reveal how you can deal with them and overcome them. Some people meeting tarot cards for the first time can be slightly nervous of them, because the images are designed to encourage your intuitive nature to respond to their messages. But the cards themselves do not invite energies or experiences into your life. They merely show you what is there already, and what this can lead into if you follow your present course of action.

Life is about choice, and self-determination. All that we experience leads to deeper self-knowledge. On the unconscious level, nothing is forgotten, and this can create patterns which influence actions we take, decisions we make, and subsequently this influences our lives. The tarot reveals the patterns, and can act as our guide for positive change. It shows the truth of who we are in the moments when we do a reading, and helps us to access our innate inner wisdom and intuition. You can view the cards as you would an old and trusted friend who shows you an accurate reflection of who you are, and gives sound and unbiased advice.

THE MAJOR ARCANA shows the journey of the soul through a series of 21 initiation processes, from I, THE MAGICIAN, to XXI, THE WORLD. These follow a sequence of archetypes, lessons, and states of being. THE FOOL card is 0, the seed, the beginning; the state of potential that gives rise to all possibilities. THE FOOL could be set at either the beginning or end of the Major Arcana, as all states are encompassed within it, but generally it is placed at the beginning as it can be seen as the first step on the journey to self-knowledge.

In a reading, the Major Arcana cards offer answers to your question, and guides as to the lessons you are learning. The cards also invite you to reflect upon the archetypes that come up in your reading, and to see how you can relate to them and understand how their energy is contained within yourself.

THE COURT CARDS, the Kings, Queens, Knights, and Maids, usually show people who are having an influence on your life. They reveal what you are learning, and which qualities either you or the people around you are embodying.

THE MINOR ARCANA show the smaller lessons taking place in our lives, and how we experience them, deal with them, and integrate them. The Minor Arcana are divided into four suits, related to the elements, numbered from 1 (the Ace) to 10.

STAFFS relate to the element of Fire. These show energy in the situation, both general and sexual energy. In terms of duality, you could view the Staffs as relating to the male qualities of energy (in both men and women) The symbol can be seen as phallic. They are active and dynamic. Fire illuminates, warms, inspires, can consume and transform, and these qualities are present in that suit, along with the perception and insight to precipitate action. Staffs relate astrologically to the Fire Signs - Aries, Leo and Sagittarius.

CHALICES relate to the element of water. In duality, the Chalices are yin/female to the yang/male of the Staffs. The Chalices show where we are receptive and intuitive, and how we interact in relationship to the self and others. Water reflects, softens, changes shape to accommodate any container; water flows, and is able to transform into ice or steam depending on the temperature it is kept at. Flowing water is healthy for us; stagnant water breeds disease, and the Chalices show what you are feeling deep within yourself, and what that is attracting into your life. Chalices relate astrologically to the Water signs - Cancer, Scorpio and Pisces.

SWORDS relate to the element of air. Air reflects our mental and spiritual processes, and the transmission of our thought-forms. Swords show how you are dealing with a situation mentally and logically, and what the spiritual lesson is. Swords are also related to meditation, to the quest of the mind for stillness; and to the sharp, penetrative insights that provoke a deep process of "seeing" and understanding. These cards can reveal how we are directing our lives, consciously and unconsciously, and whether we need to cleave to a situation, or cut through it. Swords relate to the Air signs astrologically - Gemini, Libra and Aquarius.

VESICAS relate to the element of Earth. These show our roots, our grounding in the physical aspect of ourselves. The earth nurtures, fertilises, cradles, nourishes us, and also takes our bodies back into herself at physical death. The Earth cards show what is present physically in our lives - health, wealth, poverty, possessions - and the material aspects of what we are experiencing are a reflection of what we are learning on a spiritual level.

The Vesica Pisces has been chosen as the Earth symbol for this Glastonbury Tarot. Its symbol is exquisitely wrought on the cover of Chalice Well, designed by Bligh Bond, and for that reason is associated by some with the Water element. However, the symbol of two interlocking circles represents the union of spirit and matter, consciousness and unconsciousness, and indicates the grounding of spiritual energy. Many churches and sacred sites, including Glastonbury Abbey and Stonehenge, are based on the geometry of this symbol. In a reading, the Vesicas show our dealings with the physical, the material, and how we are expressing these aspects in our lives. Astrologically, the Vesicas relate to the earth signs - Taurus, Virgo and Capricorn.

CHAPTER TWO

HOW TO USE YOUR TAROT CARDS

When you remove your tarot cards from the box for the first time, take a while to hold them in your hands in a relaxed manner. Look at the image on the back of the cards. It is of Glastonbury Tor at sunrise, the beginning of a new day and a new journey of exploration. Allow yourself to absorb the colours, and focus your mind on what you will learn from the symbolism of the images within the cards. Open yourself to your own deep, innate wisdom, and know that the answers to all questions are within you, waiting to be brought to your conscious mind through your focus on the cards. Then take your time to look at the cards one by one, and think about what each image tells you. The images have been kept as simple and uncluttered as possible so that their messages will be clear, and easy to understand.

Once you have looked at all the cards, spread them before you on a clean piece of fabric - a silk scarf is best, but any fabric will do. Silk keeps the cards clean, and also helps to keep your personal vibrational energy in the cards, so that readings you do will be clearer to you.

Swish the cards around, mix them thoroughly, and shuffle them. Some people prefer to cut the cards, by using the left hand to divide them into three piles, each pile to the left of the one before. Others like to cut the cards once, and yet others prefer to take cards straight from the pack after shuffling. The method you use isn't important; it's more a matter of being consistent once you have found the way that feels right for you. Remember, the cards themselves are not magic - it is you who are choosing, on an unconscious level, the ones that you need.

Now take one card, and look at the image. Observe the colours - what is your response to them? View the image as a story, and think about what that story could be. How do you feel, looking at the card? Once you have explored this, look up the card in the text, and see how this corresponds with your own impressions. As you use the cards over a period of time, you will find that they each have their own story for you - this book is a guide only.

Before you do a reading with your cards, it is important to be focused clearly on the question you wish to ask. The tarot cannot give answers to ambiguous questions - though you may find that it reflects another issue back at you through the cards you choose. Think about how to phrase your question. "Should I do this, or this?" will not give you a clear answer if you are making a decision. But you can ask, "What is the energy around this issue?" separately. Keep the question as straightforward and simple as possible.

You can pull out one card for an answer, or you can do a tarot spread. Or you can pull a card to ask what energy you are expressing or attracting at the moment. Here are some sample spreads that are designed to answer particular types of questions. As you experiment with the tarot, you will discover others that work for you, and you will develop particular favourites.

THE BIRD SPREAD

Can be used with 7 cards, or 8 if you wish to choose an extra one for an overall view of the situation.

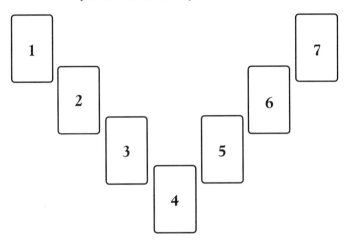

Card 1 is the present situation. It shows how you are feeling at the moment, and what is on your mind. It can also show you the question.

Card 2 indicates the factors which are influencing you, and what is happening around you.

Card 3 is the direction you need to take in order to resolve any problems.

Card 4 is the outcome - what the present course of action is likely to lead into.

Card 5 is unexpected influences coming into your life, which will have a bearing on the situation.

Card 6 is help you can obtain to find your solution, from within yourself or from others around you.

Card 7 is the future outcome, the effect that following the present course of action will have on your life.

If you want any extra clarification, you can draw an extra card, asking for an overall view of the reading.

THREE CARD SPREAD

If you want to do a quick reading for an overview of what is influencing a particular issue in your life, you can use a three-card spread.

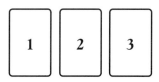

Card 1 is the past influences which have a bearing on your question.
Card 2 is the energy available to you at the moment.
Card 3 is what this is likely to lead into in the near future.

Another method of using the three-card spread is helpful:

Card 1 is where you are at the moment.
Card 2 is the obstacle or challenge facing you.
Card 3 is the solution to that obstacle.

Because relationships are an issue that most people bring to the tarot, here are two spreads that are very good for clarifying.

RELATIONSHIP SPREAD FOR COUPLES

Sit down together, and focus on your relationship, what you wish for in it, and how that can be fulfilled. Then each person selects three cards and puts them down in the order shown below.

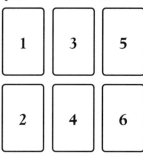

Card 1 shows how person A sees person B.
Card 2 shows how person B sees personA.
Cards 3 and 4 show obstacles to be dealt with.
Cards 5 and 6 show the direction you want the relationship to move in.

RELATIONSHIP SPREAD

This spread can give insights into a relationship you are already involved in, or one you may be contemplating. It can be used alone, or with a partner, and is helpful when discussing aspects of the relationship.

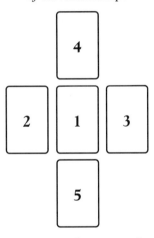

Card 1 shows where you are at the moment in the relationship.
Card 2 shows what influences have led you into it.
Card 3 shows the direction the relationship is moving in.
Card 4 shows how your partner sees you or feels about you.
Card 5 shows how you see, and feel about, your partner.

THE GLASTONBURY SPREAD: THE TREE

This spread can be used to show you the potential in your present situation, or to reveal insights into an issue.

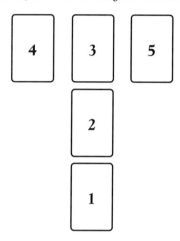

Card 1 is the seed, which contains the potential for future growth and development.
Card 2 is the root, the reality you are grounded in.
Card 3 is the trunk, the direction to follow for growth and fulfilment.
Card 4 is the branches, and what card 3 will lead you to.
Card 5 is the fruit, the culmination and outcome.

CELTIC CROSS

The next spread shown here is the Celtic Cross, which is commonly used by tarot readers, and gives a good overview of a situation.

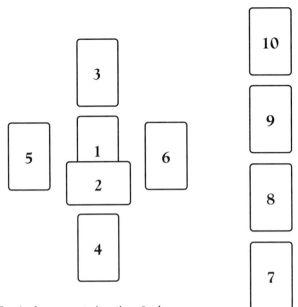

Card 1 is the present situation. It shows the atmosphere around you, and what you are dealing with.

Card 2 is the immediate influences. It shows any obstacles around you.

Card 3 is your goal, what you are aiming for.

Card 4 is the grounding, and what you are basing your question on. It can also show recent past events.

Card 5 is the past influences that have led to your present situation.

Card 6 is the near future, and the influences that you are drawing towards yourself.

Card 7 is the questioner. It shows your feelings and attitudes towards yourself.

Card 8 is the influences around you in the environment. It also reveals how other people see you.

Card 9 shows your inner emotions, your hopes and fears regarding your situation. It can also reveal things you may be keeping to yourself.

Card 10 is the final result, or outcome. It shows what your present course of action is likely to lead into.

THE ELEMENT SPREAD

The final spread is the Element Spread. The interpretation of the cards is linked in with the four cardinal directions, and the elements. It can be used for deeper insight into your inner motives if you are unclear about how you feel about an issue.

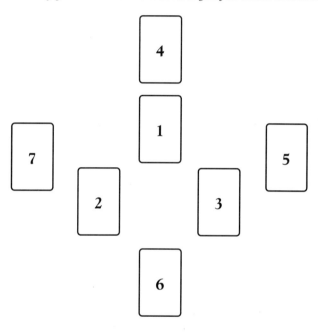

Card 1 shows what you are conscious of feeling.

Card 2 shows how you feel under the surface, or unconsciously.

Card 3 shows the direction to move your energy in.

Card 4 is the North position - the area of manifestation. It shows you what action to take.

Card 5 is the East position - what your thoughts are, and where to begin on your solution.

Card 6 is the South position. It shows what the spiritual lesson is, and also what gives you passion and inspiration.

Card 7 is the West position - your emotions, and how you need to express them.

As you become more familiar with your tarot cards, you will find that you have particular favourites among the spreads, and you may wish to develop some of your own design.

When you do a reading, start by looking at all of the cards as a whole. See whether the images and colours seem to flow, or whether there is a marked contrast in the energy of the various cards. Once you have done this, take each card one at a time, and see how it feels to you, what it means to you personally on an intuitive level, before you read the interpretation in this book. Then view the cards in the spread as a sequence, as if you are reading a story - for this is what is laid before you, a story of what is going on in your life at the moment, and what it will take you towards. Write down the cards you have drawn, with your interpretations of them. It can be useful to have a notebook to keep a record of your readings in, so that you can look at them later on and see, in retrospect, other aspects that they were showing you.

The following section of this book looks at the meaning of all of the tarot cards, and explores the history behind the figures in the Major Arcana.

THE MAJOR ARCANA

THE FOOL
PERCIVAL

0
THE FOOL
PERCIVAL

Because his father and brothers, all Knights, were killed in battle, Percival was brought up in isolation with his mother in a forest in Wales. She feared that he too would follow the fate of her other menfolk, and to avert this, brought Percival up to be totally innocent of the ways of the world. She warned him that to ask questions was impolite, and this was to hinder his first opportunity of achieving the Grail.

One day, Percival chanced upon a group of Knights on horseback in the forest, and mistook them for angels, throwing himself on his knees before them. When they explained who they were, Percival begged to be allowed to join them, and to seek to become a Knight himself. He returned to his mother to bid her farewell, and left without looking back as she collapsed with grief on a bridge by their home.

After many adventures, he beheld a beautiful castle in the distance. Awestruck, he entered, and was made welcome by a mysterious King, who was badly wounded in the groin. After feasting, a procession took place before them. Three maidens passed in a line. The first bore a lance that dripped blood. The second bore a sword, and the third carried a chalice. Although curious about the meaning of this, Percival refrained from asking about it, in case it was impolite to question.

The next day when he woke, the castle had vanished, and he continued his travels, not realising that this was the Castle of Corbenic, and the question he had refrained from asking had prevented him from attaining the Grail, and healing the Wounded King and his land.

He became a Knight to King Arthur, and, though naïve and foolish at first, eventually was with Galahad and Bors when Galahad achieved the Grail at the culmination of the Grail quest.

THE IMAGE

Percival stands on Wearyall Hill, gazing in wonder at the castle on its summit, which gleams golden in the sun. He is only partially clothed, he has not taken on the layers of garments that protect us and create a barrier between the self and the rest of the world. His trousers are white, symbolising innocence, and he stands with his arms spread at his sides in wonder. The shadows are distinctly defined, giving the image a feel of the Otherworld, and there is a fairytale quality to the scene he stands before.

The sky behind the castle reflects the sunrise, the dawn of a new day, and the time of fresh beginnings. Percival is empty-handed, he brings nothing but himself, his trust and naïvety, and his openness. In his inexperience, all that he carries with him is a sense of wonder.

DIVINATORY MEANING

The Fool card is a time of new beginnings, the first step on the journey of self-discovery. It denotes an attitude of trust and innocence, even naïvety; and also a sense of wonder. The Fool dares to take risks that others would not consider, because he is fully immersed in the moment, and has no concern for consequences. In a reading, it shows these attitudes, the demeanor of one who is able to step forward blindly into the future, in a state of perfect, and blessed, trust.

In a reading, The Fool shows that you need to trust, to take a risk, to have a fresh start and leave behind past patterns of thinking or being that have held you back. It encourages you to take a leap of faith and jump joyously into the unknown.

I
THE MAGICIAN
MERLIN

Merlin was born in what is now Carmarthen, Wales. He was conceived through the union of his mother and a spirit - reputed to be a devil whose intention was to bring forth a supernatural being to work against the rise of Christianity. Because of the spirituality of his mother, the motives of the spirit were thwarted, but he retained the gifts of prophecy and magic.

Merlin's prophesies were prolific, and accurate. In a vision, he foresaw a battle of red and white dragons, and the victory of the red dragon, which symbolised the victory of the Britons over the Saxons. He predicted the death of Gorlois, Duke of Cornwall. and the begetting of a great future king, Arthur, through the union of Uther Pendragon and the wife of Gorlois, Ygerna. He enabled Uther to seduce Ygerna by using his magic to transform Uther to look like Gorlois, on the night that Gorlois met his death in battle. On that night, Arthur, the future King, was conceived.

Stonehenge was originally reputed to be a a huge stone circle called "The Giants Ring", in Ireland. Merlin travelled there with Uther, and used his powers to transport the stones to Salisbury Plain, as a tribute to the nobles slain in battle.

Merlin became advisor to Arthur, and was instrumental in

gaining from the nobles of the land, recognition of Arthur's descent as Uther and Ygerna's son, when Arthur was brought from his foster home to take his place as King. His wisdom and magic made him a powerful ally, though Arthur acted against his advice when he married Guinevere.

Merlin met his downfall through his love for Nimue (also called Viviane), one of the Damsels of the Lake, and a powerful enchantress. She did not love him, but travelled with him through Brittany and Cornwall, and learned many of his secrets. Eventually she used his own magic to entrap him. Legends say that he was shut in a cave or tomb, alive but powerless to escape, and that one day he will return.

THE IMAGE

Merlin stands in a grove of trees, reminiscent of the sacred groves of oak trees used by the Druids. He holds aloft a chalice in his right hand and a staff in his left. The chalice indicates his ability to use his intuition, and work with the power of his emotions. The staff is topped by a crystal that shows the clarity of his thoughts and the power of the mind to act as a conductor of energy. His belt buckle is a vesica, grounding his energies and enabling him to draw down spiritual energy into the physical level. At his side is a small sword, representing his ability to use the power of his thoughts and the sharpness of his mind to accomplish what he sets out to do.

Light pours down into him from above, and creates a magic circle around his feet; but it also emanates from him, and his hair, a symbol of spiritual energy, radiates vivid light, the light of a brilliant and powerful mind at work, that bears a different quality to the golden light that is all around him. He is a picture of the will, of supreme confidence in his abilities, and the knowledge to use his gifts to their fullest.

DIVINATORY MEANING

The Magician represents the power of the will to manifest the energy needed for your purposes. It shows that you have all the tools you need at your disposal, and that you only need to have confidence in order to attain what you desire.

The Magician shows that you have a particular direction that you need to follow, and that this has deep meaning for you. It can be accomplished, with the correct focus. In the image, Merlin does not need to do anything - he simply is himself, with a strong awareness of his ability to manifest his wants and needs. He receives the power needed through the chalice and vesica, and directs it through the staff and sword. Whereas The Fool is the beginning, the Magician represents the first steps actually taken to begin a new and exciting phase of your life. It is the feeling of empowerment that you feel when you realise that you are in control of your life.

In a reading, The Magician shows that you are able to accomplish what you want through being focused on your goal. It shows strength of will and determination, and reminds you that you have all that you need at your disposal. It can also indicate someone in your life who bears these qualities.

THE HIGH PRIESTESS
MORGANA

II
THE HIGH PRIESTESS
MORGANA

Morgana, also known as Morgan le Fay and Morgaine, was the daughter of Ygerna and Gorlois, and half sister to King Arthur. After the death of Gorlois and the subsequent marriage of Ygerna and Uther and birth of Arthur, Morgana was educated in a convent and later studied under Merlin.

She lived on the magical Isle Of Avalon, and became leader and Priestess of the sisterhood there. Some myths state that it was Morgana and not Morgause, her aunt, who was mated with Arthur at the Hieros Gamos, the Sacred Marriage that joined Arthur with the land, Pagan tradition, and Fairy Folk. In this case, it would signify that Morgana was the mother of Arthur's son, Mordred, who eventually was to bring about his downfall and death.

Morgana was beautiful, intelligent, and skilled in healing and the magical arts. Her relationship with Arthur was a combination of love, betrayal, and ultimately healing. Stories told about Morgana and Arthur read like a series of tests and initiations. She married Urien, a lesser king under Arthur's rule, and bore him a son, but she also took lovers.

Morgana was perceived as a great wisewoman, healer and enchantress in Pre-Christian times. Her reputation as a meddler and dark witch was created through the prejudice of Christians in the middle ages who refuted the Pagan ways. In her time, Morgana was the powerful and respected Lady of the Lake.

Excalibur, Arthur's famous sword, was crafted in Avalon by the Fairy Folk, and at his death was cast back into the Lake from whence it had come. It was Morgana and Nimue who came for Arthur when he was dying, and who took him in the barge to Avalon for rest and healing, giving rise to the legend that Arthur sleeps on in Avalon, ready to awaken when the land needs him.

THE IMAGE

Morgana stands in the shallows of the Lake that divides Glastonbury and Avalon. She wears a skirt that rests on her hips, just above the base chakra of the body, signifying that although she is aware of her sexuality, she uses it in a tantric sense, to forge a deeper link with her spirituality and magical powers. Her skin shimmers blue in the light of the full moon that rises behind her, and her upper body is bare of clothes and adornments; she sees her body as an instrument of her will.

Light pours from her outstretched hands as she draws power into herself. Her feet and the hem of her skirt are immersed in the water; she understands her emotions and is able to use them, and to separate herself from them when necessary.

A veil flows down her back and across her face. Her mysteries have to be sought by seekers through a deep, inner longing, before she will allow them to be penetrated. A headdress holds her veil in place, forged of a symbol of the full moon resting on a dark moon, signifying attunement with the powers of intuition.

In the background, illuminated by the full moon, a hand rises from the water, holding aloft the magical sword, Excalibur, crafted by the Fairy Folk under the eye of the Priestesses of Avalon. This reveals the treasures that are brought to the surface through following the intuition, and the empowerment that these can bring.

DIVINATORY MEANING

The High Priestess is the consort of The Magician. Her powers are equal to his, yet different. Whereas The Magician needs the tools of the elements to work with in order to manifest his desires, the High Priestess requires nothing but her body, mind and intuition. Together, these first two figures in the tarot give rise to the third,

The Empress - the birthing process.

The High Priestess signifies the power of intuition, and the transformation that takes place once you listen to your inner voice. She symbolises an attunement with the magic and mystery inherent in every facet of life. This is not something that the logical mind can grasp - it is too intangible and elusive, yet can be known on a subtle level, and worked with. The High Priestess encourages you to follow your inner feelings, and ignore the voice of the mind. To enter the mystery hidden behind her veil, we need to surrender rationality, withdraw our tendencies to look at what is on the surface, and allow ourselves to listen to our feelings.

This card tells you to follow your intuition, and to understand that, if you act on it, you will be enabled to understand aspects of your situation that could not be seen or understood previously.

III
THE EMPRESS
GUINEVERE

Guinevere, also known as Gwenhywfar, was the daughter of Leodegan, and was descended of Roman blood. She was famed for her beauty, and King Arthur fell in love with her and took her as his wife. An inscription on their grave in Glastonbury Abbey in the Middle Ages calls Guinevere Arthur's second wife, and some myths state that there were actually three Guineveres. This may be related to the Pagan Triple Goddess - the Maiden, Mother and Crone, as the Queen of the land at Guinevere and Arthur's time was viewed as more than a consort to the King. She represented the health and vitality of the earth itself, and in Medieval times the queen needed to be a strong woman who was seen to go her own way. Because of this, Guinevere's unfaithfulness did not detract from Arthur's image as a just and wise King, whose legends were to live on through the ages.

Merlin was opposed to the marriage of Arthur and Guinevere, but Arthur went ahead with the marriage, and stayed in love with his wife throughout their time together. Guinevere was linked with men other than her husband, and this brought disaster on him. She was abducted by Melwas, King of the Summerland (Somerset), and kept at a castle on Glastonbury Tor until Arthur arrived armed for battle, and Melwas capitulated. Some legends tell that Lancelot rescued her from the clutches of Melwas, and that this was the true starting point for their affair. Guinevere's love affair with Lancelot lasted through most of Arthur's reign, and was brought to Arthur's attention through a potion made by Morgana which, on drinking, brought clear vision. There was also reputed to be a sexual liaison between Guinevere and Mordred, Arthur's son, which created the final rift between them that led to the death of Arthur at Mordred's hand.

When Guinevere's relationship with Lancelot was made public by Mordred, it was seen as treason, and Arthur reluctantly condemned Guinevere to be burnt at the stake. She was rescued by Lancelot and entered a convent, but this divided the Round Table and brought about Arthur's downfall, leading eventually to the quest for the Grail to heal the King and the land.

THE IMAGE

Guinevere sits on the grass in a meadow, surrounded by wild flowers. Behind her is the ancient hill-fort of South Cadbury, which is believed to be the site of Camelot. The sun shines over the land and all looks peaceful and verdant. Guinevere sits with her right hand resting on the earth, acting as an anchor for her energy. Her close link with the land is evident in that she does not place any cloth or blanket beneath her to create a barrier. She sits cross-legged, she is able to contain her energy within herself. Yet her outstretched hand shows that she gives freely of herself, and, like the land itself, holds nothing back.

Guinevere's dress is a vibrant cerise pink, the colour of love in its highest expression, relating to the heart and to the womb - woman's centre of gravity. Her undergarment, visible within her sleeves, is a light green, relating to the heart energy and to balance and creativity. She is a powerful embodiment of Woman in her role as Goddess of the land. Her hair flows freely down her back, unfettered, and is the colour of the corn that gives nourishment. The hair is also a symbol for allowing the expression of the spiritual aspect of the Self.

Her left hand, the hand of receptiveness and intuition, is extended, and all of her attention is focused on the butterfly that is about to alight on her hand. The butterfly represents transformation, the alchemy that takes place when you are able to go deep

44

within the self and emerge with a full realisation of who and what you are.

A tree stands at the side of the image, showing Guinevere's total connection with the land. The roots of a tree can spread as far and wide beneath the earth as its branches spread in the sky. This embodies the ability to endure, to exist at all levels of your being, and to be attuned to the seasons of your life as well as the seasons of the year.

DIVINATORY MEANING

The Empress card symbolises the energy of a full-blooded woman, a lover and mother figure. Whereas The High Priestess connects us with the intuitive, subtle aspects of femininity that can seem almost intangible, and with the expression of the mind into form, The Empress is the power of woman that is firmly earthed and anchored, that is passionately emotional, and has strong needs and desires that can override reason.

The marriage of Card I, the will , and Card II, the inner power, creates Card III, a state of harmony, and a synthesis, a new creative and procreative energy. The Empress can be seen as the union of The Magician and The High Priestess, the child that is brought into being. In a reading, this can signify a physical child, or the birth of an idea or vision that can now be nurtured.

The Empress symbolises a time of growth, a harmonising process, and the birth of fresh and exciting energy in your life. It is the feeling of passion, of being prepared to give all that you have to whatever you are involved in. You are likely to be feeling an urge to indulge yourself, and to create pleasure for those around you. This card teaches you how to connect with your emotions, and allow yourself to truly feel them and express them. It also signifies an upsurge of creativity that could prove to be beneficial in both the material and emotional areas of your life.

IV
THE EMPEROR
ARTHUR

The birth of Arthur, and his destiny as King, were prophesied by Merlin, who also played a magical role in the proceedings. Uther, Arthur's future father, fell in love with Ygerna, who was at the time married to Gorlois. Seeing this, Gorlois swiftly left Uther's court without permission, and fled to Tintagel, which gave Uther an excuse to make war on him.

Merlin accompanied Uther and his men to Tintagel, and used a spell to transform Uther into a likeness of Gorlois, in order that he might enter Tintagel castle and seduce Ygerna. That night, Arthur was conceived, and Gorlois was killed in battle, leaving Ygerna free to marry Uther.

After Arthur's birth, Merlin took him from his parents to be fostered with Ector, a rich knight, and his sons. Arthur grew up unaware of his true parentage.

When Uther died, the land was thrown into confusion, with no King named to take his place. An assembly of Knights was called to find a new ruler, and Merlin placed a sword in a stone, and declared that whoever could remove it would be King. Many tried, to no avail, until eventually the young Arthur attempted it, and removed the sword effortlessly. He was declared King, and was recognised as the son of Uther and Ygerna.

Not long after his reign, the sword broke, and Merlin took Arthur to a lake, where he watched in awe as an arm holding aloft a sword rose above the water. This was Excalibur, the famous sword that was forged magically by the Faery-Folk, at the behest of the Ladies of Avalon. Its scabbard had the power to stop bleeding wounds, and to heal the bearer, and the sword was the indestructible slayer of enemies.

Arthur was a Christian King, but was also tolerant of, and sympathetic to the Pagan religion, which still bore influence across the land. When he was crowned King, he also underwent the Hieros Gamos, the Sacred Marriage to the land, in order to be recognised by the Pagans and the Faery Folk. He bore Christian images into battle, yet wielded Excalibur, and honoured the magical process which had constructed it as an instrument of power. He took as an emblem on his shield a depiction of a vision he had at the Beckery, a convent in Glastonbury, of the Virgin Mary and baby Jesus. He was unbeatable in battle, and legends abound of the heroic exploits of Arthur and his Knights.

Arthur married Guinevere, and as part of her dowry was given a round table. He used this as a meeting point for himself and his Knights, so that all would be seen as equal. Later, Merlin was to forge another table, the Round Table of legend.

Arthur had no children with Guinevere, but fathered Mordred, his son and eventual nemesis, at his Sacred Marriage with the land at his crowning. The mother was either Morgana, his half-sister whom he had not met since infancy, or Morgause, his aunt; and though he was innocent of their blood relationship when the union took place, once he knew of it, it shamed him. He also bore two other illegitimate sons, who both died young.

There are many tales of King Arthur. One tells of Arthur's journey into the Underworld to the land of Annwn, to steal the magical cauldron of nourishment. Merlin foretold of Arthur coming as the Boar, and he is also associated with the Bear Constellation, because the Roman version of his name, Arturus, means 'Bear'.

Arthur's reign brought peace to a land that had been torn by conflict, until the rift between himself and his beloved knight Lancelot, due to Lancelot's affair with Guinevere, divided the Round Table and scattered the Knights in pursuit of the Grail. Many of them died on the quest, but the Grail was eventually attained by

Galahad, the son of Lancelot and Elaine, accompanied by Percival and Bors.

Arthur was at war in Gaul when he heard that Mordred, whom he had left in charge of Guinevere and his land in his absence, had attempted to seize the crown and take Guinevere as his wife. Swiftly he returned, and in the battle, Mordred dealt Arthur a mortal blow, and was killed himself as Arthur fell. The magical scabbard of Excalibur which had the power to heal wounds had been stolen, so Arthur was helpless. Knowing that he was dying, Arthur ordered Bedivere to throw Excalibur into the Lake. Twice Bedivere could not do this. On the third attempt, Bedivere watched as the hand of the Lady of the Lake rose up to grasp the sword, and vanish with it beneath the water.

The Barge of Avalon crossed the water, carrying Morgana and Nimue, who, weeping, took the body of Arthur back with them to Avalon for healing. Legends say that he rests there still, waiting to return when the land needs him.

THE IMAGE

King Arthur sits on a throne which bears carved rams' horns, revealing the leadership qualities of the astrological sign Aries, which rules the card. Aries stands for leadership qualities, great dynamism and energy which can accomplish a great deal, a tremendous love of life, and the ability to tap into personal power. The throne is gold, the colour of spiritual energy, and this is reflected in the leggings Arthur wears, denoting that he is aware of that energy, and able to use it - to 'walk his talk'.

The throne is situated at the roots of a tree in Wick Hollow, Glastonbury. The roots protrude from the earth and create caves and hollows in the banks that flank that area. It is an appropriate setting for The Emperor, who symbolises stability and form, the relationship to the physical aspects of life, and the ability to be rooted in the present. The negative aspect of The Emperor is a tendency to live in the past, and to enforce his ideas on others, in a misuse of personal power.

The base of the throne is covered by a purple cloth. Purple is the colour of rulership. In olden times, dyes of that colour were so expensive to extract that only royalty and some of the priesthood were able to wear that colour. It also relates to the 7th chakra, on the crown of the head, which governs the spiritual aspect of the Self.

Arthur was viewed as the spiritual as well as the temporal ruler of the land.

Arthur wears a deep crimson tunic, emphasising his kingly qualities. On it are embroidered two dragons in battle, one red and one white. These were seen in a vision by Merlin before Arthur's birth, and represented the victory of the Britons against the Saxons. Until the end of his reign, Arthur was seen to be invincible.

Across his lap, Arthur loosely balances a sceptre that also bears the symbol of a ram's head. It indicates that he was able to rule with a firm and just hand, without abusing the authority of his position. His sword, Excalibur, rests at his side. It is close enough to be grasped instantly if necessary, but the fact that it stands alone shows that he does not depend on force to achieve all of his aims. The sword is there, and ready, when he needs it. Excalibur's point is balanced on the earth - the kingly qualities and energies are firmly grounded.

Arthur's legs are crossed at the ankles, symbolising that he is able to contain his energy within himself, and so has a strong foundation to build his power upon. His face is serene, and he gazes directly out of the image into the eyes of the observer. There is an aura of benevolence emanating from him, and a sense of knowing who and what he is, without arrogance. He seems to be waiting, as if to listen to, and answer your question.

DIVINATORY MEANING

In a reading, The Emperor signifies stability and authority. There is the need, and the ability, to maintain the status quo, and to act as an anchor. Whereas The Empress is the Mother figure, the fount of creativity and passion, The Emperor is the Father figure, who is able to lay the groundwork for that creativity to rest upon and spring from. The Emperor lays foundations, creates boundaries, stability and order, enforces discipline, and analyses using the rational mind.

This card means that these qualities are present in yourself, or someone close to you. It denotes a need to focus on these qualities, to see them in yourself and to express them more in your life. The negative aspect of The Emperor is rigidity, too strong a need for structure and rules, which can be stifling. This should be guarded against. Generally, The Emperor signifies a strong, grounded person with an air of authority and charismatic personal power.

V
THE HIEROPHANT
JOSEPH OF ARIMATHEA

Joseph of Arimathea was a tin merchant, and the uncle of Jesus. He travelled widely, and visited Cornwall and Glastonbury. Some say that Jesus accompanied Joseph on his travels as a young man, and that the first church in the Western Isles, a small round hut on the future site of Glastonbury Abbey, was built by Jesus, though other legends attribute it to Joseph.

After the crucifixion of Jesus, it was Joseph of Arimathea who laid his body in the tomb. He was said to have kept two cruets, one containing the blood and the other the sweat of Christ; and the chalice, or cup, used by Jesus at the Last Supper.

Joseph travelled to Gaul, then England, and arrived by boat at Wearyall Hill, Glastonbury - so-called because all who arrived here were weary, and could rest. Stepping onto Wearyall Hill, Joseph drove his staff into the ground, where it took root and blossomed, to become the famous Glastonbury Thorn tree which grows nowhere else in this country, and flowers every Christmas.

The King of this area at that time was Arviragus, a Druid. Although he never converted to Christianity, he was sympathetic towards Joseph and his followers, and gave them twelve hides of land, upon which the first Christian churches were built. These took

the form of small round huts, and for the rest of their lives, Joseph
and his followers lived and taught there.

THE IMAGE

Joseph stands before the first Christian church, sited on the land
upon which the future Glastonbury Abbey was built. The majestic
Abbey ruins still stand, a monument to the grandeur of the vision of
its builders.

Joseph is shown talking to his young disciples, and his left hand
is extended in a gesture of offering as he makes a point in his
discourse. His face is kind, and wise, deeply etched with the lines
created by laughter, suffering, acceptance and wisdom. He has lived
through a great many experiences, and through his integration of
these, has undergone a deep transformation within himself. He has
willingly taken on the role of spiritual guide and teacher, in order to
spread his wisdom and convey his insights to others.

Joseph's robe is white; he has renounced the material aspects of
life and is now focused on the Spiritual. Around his head is a
nimbus of light; he radiates knowledge and wisdom. He carries a
staff similar to the one that he planted in the earth at Wearyall Hill.

The three disciples represent the trinity of body, mind and spirit,
and the alchemical union between all of these which must take place
in order to facilitate the merging of the small self with the higher
Self. It is this sense of merging which gives rise to the blissful states
of awareness and unity, which The Hierophant is attempting to
convey to his followers. The disciples wear brown cloaks, wrapped
snugly around themselves, indicating the grounding of the words
and ideas conveyed to them by Joseph, and that they are hugging
those words close in order to understand them.

DIVINATORY MEANING

The Hierophant is the spiritual teacher, the wise one from whom
you can seek advice, and who is able to give you what you need
(though that may not always be the same as what you want). In a
reading, this can be someone from whom you can seek guidance, or
it can mean that you should now tap into this aspect of yourself and
listen to what your heart and head are telling you. The Emperor
oversees the temporal, physical well-being of his subjects; he
protects them and gives them the guidelines for daily living. The
Hierophant takes this further, and focuses on the spiritual well-

being that helps the soul become aware of its path through eternity.

The Hierophant card signifies a step forward on your spiritual path. It can show an adherence to a particular philosophy which acts as a guide for your life. Yet the Hierophant does not mean that you should seek a guru who will allow you to hand over responsibility for your life. A true spiritual teacher will always encourage you to seek the answers deep within yourself. This card shows that all the answers are here within you, and if you pay attention to the messages of others, then look deep inside your own heart, the answers you seek will be there.

The Hierophant represents your willingness to take responsibility for yourself on all levels of being.

THE LOVERS
CREIDDYLAD AND GWYTHYR

VI
THE LOVERS
CREIDDYLAD AND GWYTHYR

The tale of Creiddylad, daughter of Lludd Silver-Hand, and Gwythyr, son of Greidawl, is a story of the union of the Earth Goddess and the Sun God. The golden-haired beauty of Creiddylad, and her goodness, marked her out as consort to Gwythyr, and the couple joyfully prepared for their wedding. But Gwyn Ap Nudd, King of the Faeries and Lord of the Underworld, who lived beneath Glastonbury Tor, also fell in love with Creiddylad, and he plotted to take her as his wife.

At the Celtic Spring Festival of Beltane, Creiddylad and Gwythyr moved in a procession of villagers to the top of the Tor, where they consummated their union in order to bring fertility to the land. Their wedding was close at hand, and they were deeply in love.

Gwyn tricked Gwythyr with false messages, so that he could disguise himself, using his magic, as Gwythyr. Creiddylad penetrated his disguise, and refused to go with him, and in his rage, Gwyn revealed his true identity and was banished by King Arthur. Humiliated and furious, Gwyn abducted Creiddylad by force, and when Gwythyr and his men set off in pursuit, captured all but Gwythyr.

The Mabinogion tells that Arthur insisted that neither man could wed Creiddylad, and she was returned to the house of her father, where she lived out her days. But another story relates how Creiddylad was imprisoned by Gwyn in the tunnels beneath the Tor, until eventually Gwythyr, with the help of St. Collen, rescued her and vanquished Gwyn Ap Nudd.

Each Beltane sunrise, it is told that a battle takes place on top of the Tor, between Gwyn Ap Nudd and Gwythyr for the love of Creiddylad.

THE IMAGE

Creiddylad and Gwythyr stand close together against the sunset. Behind them, a full moon, representing the time when the emotions are at their height, and a time of blossoming, rises above the pink and gold sky. A branch of cherry blossom leans towards them, and Creiddylad wears a circlet of cherry blossom in her hair - a flower traditionally associated with romance and weddings.

Creiddylad stands before Gwythyr who holds her in a close embrace. Her hands reach up to hold his, and the shape created by their arms forms two runic symbols - the rune of transformation, which is shaped like a butterfly, and the rune for a gift, which forms an X shape. The rune of transformation, Daeg, symbolises a new influx of energy, the ability to endure over a period of time, and a major breakthrough which facilitates a new beginning. The rune of the gift, Gebo, is also the symbol for a kiss, and denotes the union of the self, through love, with the divine.

Gwythyr wears a deep blue, almost indigo, tunic, and blue leggings. These reveal his devotion to Creiddylad, and to the ideal of Love as a force for change. Around his head is a circlet of leaves, reflecting his connection with the earth and the sky - leaves are anchored to the trees, yet are also suspended in the air.

Creiddylad wears an apple green dress, the colour of healing and of heart energy. Her inner robe is coloured in the same shades of blue as Gwythyr's clothes, signifying that their devotion to each other is connected with, and fundamental to, their spiritual nature.

Their faces are serene, almost serious. They are aware that love brings with it trials and responsibilities, and are willing to experience all aspects of it. Theirs is no mere infatuation, it is a bond that endures, whatever pain and pleasure that may bring them.

DIVINATORY MEANING

Once the lessons of The Hierophant have been learned, those of understanding the spiritual nature of the Self, being able to communicate, and the ability to take responsibility for oneself, the journey of The Fool moves on to understanding the Self through union with another. Often, we can learn more about ourselves through a relationship than is possible alone, as the other person acts as a mirror for us. We tend to be attracted to people who either reflect aspects of ourselves back at us, or who seem to have qualities which we feel that we lack, and which we desire.

Interestingly, although we may have a physical ideal of a partner, the attraction principle is actually a chemical reaction which takes place in the nose, which picks up the pheromones of the other person, and reacts strongly. This may not seem very romantic, but it illustrates that attraction, and love, is based upon something extremely subtle, which 'sniffs out' the person who is right for us.

The Lovers card represents a lover either in your life at the moment, or about to enter your life. It also signifies a choice that you need to make. This can be between two prospective partners, or the choice as to whether to explore the possibilities of a relationship, or to remain alone in order to discover the male and female aspects of yourself.

The Lovers card has its dark side as well. Gwyn Ap Nudd attempted to steal Creiddylad away from Gwythyr, and this can be taken symbolically to mean that there can be a danger of immersing yourself so deeply in the relationship that you forget who you are, and submerge your needs in order to satisfy those of another. The urge to merge with another person reflects a higher desire to merge with the Self, and experience an orgasmic sense of Unity - but it is important that our sense of identity and individuality is retained.

The Lovers card is about duality - the polarity of male and female. The dark and light aspects of ourselves come to the surface in a relationship. This card signifies a willingness to experience the joy and the pain, the sense of unity and the sense of estrangement, in the quest for personal growth. It shows that the opportunity is present for an exciting relationship in your life, which will teach you a great deal about yourself.

THE CHARIOT
THE BARGE OF AVALON

VII
THE CHARIOT
THE BARGE OF AVALON

Myths tell that Glastonbury and Avalon are joined so that they seem to be one and the same place - but that Avalon exists on a different plane, or level, to Glastonbury. The powerful magical energy of Avalon is strongly associated with Glastonbury; perhaps its proximity allows the energy to flow, or leak, into Glastonbury. Or perhaps Glastonbury expresses the energy of Avalon in a more material form.

Originally Glastonbury was surrounded by water, and the Tor rose above the little islands that dotted what is now the Somerset Levels. It was a place of mystery, said to be haunted, and seen as home to the Faery Folk, the ancient and wise beings who shunned human contact.

Avalon was a magical island, scented with apple blossom, a place of healing and secrecy that was home to the Priestesses. Few mortals travelled there, though many lost their way in the marshes searching for it. The only way that Avalon could be accessed was in a barge that was guided by the will of a Priestess. This meant that only those who were invited to Avalon were able to see this beautiful and mysterious place.

It was thought that Avalon was a mirror-image of Glastonbury.

Buildings excavated on the Tor date back to the fifth or sixth century C. E., so it is possible that a small church existed on top of the Tor from those times. But the Tor in Avalon was reputed to be topped by a circle of standing stones, or trees. In Avalon, the Priestesses lived in harmony with the Faery Folk and with nature. They were able to develop their skills in magic and healing, and to maintain their privacy and sense of mystery.

THE IMAGE

Viviane, one of the Ladies of the Lake, stands calmly in the barge as it moves away from Glastonbury towards Avalon. In the distance, the Tor and several small islands rise above the water.

Viviane's demeanour is relaxed, yet her bearing is proud and erect. Her hands are hidden in the folds of her cloak. There are no oars, or any visible way of guiding the vessel. She directs the course of the barge using the power of her will, as there is no physical way into Avalon, the land of the spirit, which can take her there. It is attained through a change in consciousness. She knows that the power of the mind can be stronger than that of the body, and that the body and mind are both subject to the force of the will.

The setting sun casts gleaming light upon the water, and reflects the golden colour of the barge - the colour of the Will and the Spirit. The barge is illuminated from within by a combination of light of its own and from the Priestess, which shimmers on the bottom of her cloak. At its prow is set a silver moon, in the shape which symbolises the dark moon, the time when dreams and visions can be at their most potent because they come from the depths of the unconscious.

Viviane's cloak is of a rich, deep blue-green. She understands her emotions and is able to rise above them. This also represents her powers as a healer, and her ability to tap deep into the mysteries of life. At her throat, area of communication, is a clasp in the shape of the lemniscate, showing her awareness of the eternal nature of life. She also wears a moonstone at her throat, a stone reputed to heighten the power of intuition, and related to the astrological sign Cancer, which rules this card. Her dress is the blue of devotion to a spiritual ideal, and it hangs in loose folds to show that she is able to be fluid in her thinking, and to respect the philosophies of others even if they are not in accordance with her own.

Her lips are a deep red. This is a person who is able to relate on all levels of her being. Her energies are primarily concerned with the spiritual, but there is also room in her life and her nature for passion if it serves her higher good. Relationships are only important to her if they also have a spiritual foundation. Viviane's refusal to be Merlin's lover was primarily because she was repulsed by the idea that his father was said to be a demon.

The barge seems to glide through the water so smoothly that it barely creates any ripples; it seems almost to be floating. When the will is strong, nothing is able to stand in its way, and obstacles seem to be greatly lessened, almost to disappear.

DIVINATORY MEANING

The Chariot represents purposeful control of the senses by the Will. In The Lovers, the lesson was learned through relationship with another. The Chariot shows that this lesson has been absorbed, the youthful energy of The Lovers has developed into a state of maturity, with the knowledge that we can guide and direct our lives, and that only we ourselves are able to know what we truly want, and manifest it. The Chariot represents a state of increasing confidence, which attracts success in our endeavours.

In a reading, this card shows that you are able to control your situation through the focus of the will. It is a time of success and victory over obstacles. The Chariot represents new and positive beginnings. You are moving into a new dimension of life, a change for the better, a fresh phase. This could be a new job, relationship, or home, and it brings with it a feeling of excitement and renewal.

The Chariot also signifies the ability to look deep within yourself, and to be guided by your intuition. There is a need to tie up any loose ends in your life so that you can move forward freely.

The element of control personified by this card cautions against using personal power to manipulate others. One of the essential components of life is free will - the knowledge that we are able to an extent to shape our destiny. However, the Cancerian element in The Chariot also indicates a sensitivity to the needs and feelings of others.

VIII
JUSTICE
ARVIRAGUS

Arviragus was King of Britain in the first century CE. He was the younger son of Cymbeline, a much respected King who was on good terms with Rome. When Cymbeline died he was succeeded by the elder brother of Arviragus, Guiderius, but the goodwill of Rome ceased when Guiderius stopped paying tribute. The Emperor Claudius invaded Britain, Guiderius was killed, and Arviragus succeeded to the throne.

Arviragus, a Druid, proved to be a fearsome opponent - the Druids were powerfully opposed to Roman rule. So Claudius, knowing that he would lose in battle, negotiated a treaty with Arviragus, in which Britain was still dependent on Rome, but retained self-rule. Arviragus married the daughter of Claudius, Genuissa, but refused any further homage to Rome. A battle was fought at Exeter, halted by the arrival of Genuissa, and her intercession led to a treaty. Arviragus ruled peacefully for the rest of his life, and was known as a wise and just king. He was buried in Gloucester - some say that he was laid to rest at the site of a temple he had built to Claudius, but in view of the temperament of the Druids, it is unlikely that he would have built a temple to the Emperor of Rome.

It was while Arviragus was King that Joseph of Arimathea, uncle of Jesus, sailed to Glastonbury after the death of Jesus. (See card V, The Hierophant). Arviragus treated him with respect, and, although not converted to Christianity himself, bequeathed to Joseph twelve hides of land on which to build the first Christian churches.

THE IMAGE

Arviragus stands in a grove of trees, which glow with the green light of balance. Behind him, the light is a deep purple at ground level, symbolising his kingly qualities, rising to the blues of wisdom and devotion to a spiritual ideal. This shows his ability to think and see clearly, and to communicate his knowledge.

Arviragus looks strong and uncompromising. He stands full-square, keeping his centre of balance, and holds a wooden pole on which are suspended two bowls in perfect balance. One bowl is silver, symbolising the moon, the ability to follow the intuition and to know truths from the depths of feeling. The other bowl is of gold, representing the solar energy - the ability to deduce logically, to calculate the rights and wrongs in a situation. Together, they form an image of a state of balanced perfection in a human being, one who is able to access all aspects of his being in order to come to a solution.

Arviragus also bears aspects of the wild man. He looks regal and proud, but also untamed - his instincts are strong, and he follows them. He wears a deerskin cloak, denoting that he is in touch with the energies of nature. The deer also symbolises gentleness, and the ability to listen to others. Around his neck is a golden torc, indicating his royal heritage. At his throat, clasping his cloak is a brooch engraved with a spiral, and this is repeated on his belt. The spiral symbolises the knowledge that life is eternal, and moves in cycles - he is able to communicate this (the throat) and feel this at the centre of his being, the solar plexus.

His tunic is blue, the colour of devotion and rulership, and his leggings are yellow, revealing that his mental processes are clear. On his fingers are tattooed blue spirals that wind downwards into snakes, the symbol of wisdom. A dark moon is tattooed on his forehead, indicating his connection with the psychic elements of himself.

DIVINATORY MEANING

The Justice card moves you onward from the ability to use the will represented by The Chariot, to the ability to see all sides of a situation in order to know the right choices to make or paths to take. Justice implies accepting responsibility for yourself, and in doing so we are able to free ourselves of past patterns of behaviour that would otherwise be constantly repeated. This card shows that every action has a re-action, and leads to the realisation that we are the sum of our past experiences, yet also have the ability to change the way we view ourselves and the world, and to see clearly how the choices we make will affect what energy comes into our lives. This is not to say that we can control every aspect of our lives - that is impossible, as too many outside influences affect us. Yet it does teach us that we can begin to truly know ourselves, and discover what serves our higher purpose.

The Justice card in a reading indicates honesty, and fair dealings with others. It shows the ability to see both sides of a situation. It can also mean a just decision being made about your life - though it may or may not be what you want, it will be the right decision for you.

This card shows the need, and the ability, to seek balance within yourself; to stay centred and avoid extremes that could pull you away from your centre. By following this course, you are able to attain a state of inner harmony which will act as a guide to the right course of action for you.

THE HERMIT
ST. COLLEN

IX
THE HERMIT
ST. COLLEN

St. Collen was an early Welsh saint, thought to have once been an abbot at Glastonbury Abbey. He retired to a cave on the slopes of the Tor, which could be the cave where the White Spring is now situated. Collen was skilled in healing, independent, and uncompromising. One of the tales told of him is linked in with the story of Creiddylad and Gwythyr, in card VI, The Lovers. Another legend shows his powerful belief in himself and his religion.

The Tor was the home of Gwyn Ap Nudd, the King of the Faeries and Lord of the Underworld. He lived within its depths, and he and his subjects were seen as demons and regarded with fear by the people who were adopting the Christian religion.

One day Collen overheard two men outside his cave discussing Gwyn and the Faeries. He cautioned them not to pay these demons any attention, and the men replied that he had now offended Gwyn, who would seek retribution. Soon afterwards, a faery messenger came to invite Collen to meet with Gwyn. Collen refused. On subsequent days, the messenger returned with the same invitation, and then with threats, until eventually Collen agreed to meet Gwyn on top of the Tor.

Collen climbed the Tor, carrying hidden on his person a small vial of holy water. At its summit, he saw to his amazement a beautiful castle. On entering, he beheld many magnificently dressed men and women feasting with Gwyn at their head. Gwyn cordially invited Collen to join the feast, but Collen, knowing the danger in this, refused, and scattered holy water over the assembly. Immediately Gwyn, his courtiers and the castle all vanished, leaving Collen alone on top of the Tor. In this way, by St. Collen banishing Gwyn Ap Nudd, Christianity took over from the old religion.

THE IMAGE

St. Collen stands at the top of the Tor, holding aloft a flaming torch. This represents the light of the Self shining out, sending more light into the world. He glows with his own inner fire of inspiration; he is lit from within, and is willing to unstintingly give what he has, for the higher good of all. The figure wears a brown robe, indicating renunciation of worldly life in favour of the spiritual quest, and also symbolising that he retains his connection with the earth, and aims to use his spiritual insights in a practical way.

Around Collen's neck is a silver cross, and in his left hand he carries a pewter bottle filled with holy water. The hood of his robe is pulled up over his head, showing that he wishes to be set apart from worldly considerations. He is of the world, but not in it.

The setting sun reveals in silhouette the top of the round hut that was the first Christian church. Collen has left this behind also; his path is one of willing solitude and contemplation.

DIVINATORY MEANING

The Hermit is the spiritual guide. While the Justice card shows the ability to differentiate between right and wrong and act accordingly, the Hermit allows you to withdraw from the outer world in order to look deep within yourself. This brings about the process of awakening the awareness of the spiritual nature.

In a reading, The Hermit shows that this is a time when you need to be alone in order to explore the deeper aspects of yourself. It is a period of withdrawal from worldly considerations. This could mean a retreat, or merely a need to set aside a little time each day to just be with yourself; to think, or meditate, or read books that inspire you or make you think. To be alone is essentially to be all-one, to feel at peace with yourself.

Receiving The Hermit card does not mean that you deprive

yourself of relationships with others. However, its rulership by the astrological sign Virgo does indicate that you need to be discriminating about who shares your life, and that you feel the need to only allow close to you those people who share your ideals. This card can also signify that someone is entering your life whom you respect, and can learn a great deal from.

Perhaps you have been hiding your light under a bushel. If so, now is the time to let the beauty of your true self radiate outwards so that it can be recognised by others. Kindred spirits can then be drawn to you, who will accompany you on the next stage of your spiritual journey.

THE WHEEL OF FORTUNE
THE GLASTONBURY ZODIAC

X
THE WHEEL OF FORTUNE
THE GLASTONBURY ZODIAC

The Glastonbury Zodiac was discovered in 1925 by Katherine Maltwood, who called it "The Temple of the Stars". It lies in a circle 10 miles in diameter, from Glastonbury in the north, to Somerton in the south, and bears within its landscape the figures of the twelve signs of the zodiac in the correct order. The figures are shaped by rocks, streams and land boundaries. Glastonbury is in the area of Aquarius, represented by a phoenix, with Glastonbury Tor on the eye of the phoenix. Wearyall Hill rides the back of the whale of Pisces.

The Zodiac can only be seen in its entirety from the air, but can be walked around if a map is used - though this takes some time. It has its own myths. Some say that it dates back to around 2,700 BCE; others that it is far younger. It holds a connection with the Arthurian legends, with Sagittarius the Archer - a figure on horseback without bow and arrows - as King Arthur. His Queen, Guinevere, is represented by Virgo, and the other signs are linked in with Arthur's Knights. The circle of the Zodiac itself is said to be the legendary Round Table.

Just outside the circle sits the Great Dog Of Langport, seen as its guardian, a Cerberus-type figure. The tip of its tail marks the hamlet of Wagg, and several of the place-names situated within the Zodiac reflect their association with their particular zodiac sign or figure.

THE IMAGE

This shows the exact proportions and layout of the Glastonbury Zodiac. It begins on the left of the painting, with Aries as a lamb, its fleece the golden colour of new beginnings. Beside Aries is the head of Taurus, the Bull, with the arm of one of the twins of Gemini almost touching his muzzle. Cancer is represented as a boat rather than a crab, and its sails look almost like a figure standing holding a staff. Leo, the Lion, is rather heraldic in appearance. Around from Leo is the figure of Virgo holding a wheatsheaf.

Libra is represented by a dove, the bird of peace. It sits in the approximate centre of the Zodiac circle, symbolising the state of equilibrium that the sign Libra stands for. Scorpio, the Scorpion, reaches its pincers towards Sagittarius, the Archer, as if to nip him. It seems almost as if the rider of Sagittarius is being dragged from his horse by the teeth of the Whale. Capricorn is a Goat, but also has a similarity in appearance to a unicorn. Aquarius is a flame-feathered phoenix rising above Glastonbury, looking in the direction of Pisces, represented by a whale and two fishes.

DIVINATORY MEANING

The Wheel Of Fortune symbolises the constant cycle of change that we experience in life. There are always high points and low points, and the teaching of this card is to learn to stay centred in who you are, whatever is going on externally in your life. In the Arthurian legends, on the eve of Arthur's final battle, he dreamed of a giant wheel turned by the Goddess Fortuna, with himself crushed beneath it. This reveals that however much we may seem to be in control of our own destiny, there is always an unseen factor at work, called Fate by many, which can cause the best laid plans and the strongest confidence to go awry.

The lesson of The Hermit was to go within, to discover the power that can be gained through introspection. This leads us to The Wheel Of Fortune, of finding and maintaining our inner centre. You can picture this as an actual wheel - the spokes, which are outward experiences and influences, are kept in place by the hub at their centre, which remains undisturbed by their movement.

In a reading, The Wheel Of Fortune signifies a change coming in your life, usually for the better. Even if it does not seem to be what you want, this change will move you in a new, and perhaps surprising, direction. It indicates a breakthrough in your situation that leads to an expansion within yourself. Ensure that you stay centred, and allow yourself to go with the flow.

XI

XI
STRENGTH
GOG AND MAGOG

Gog and Magog are two ancient oak trees, at least 1,000 years old, which still leaf every summer. They are named after a legendary Cornish giant, said to be 18 feet tall, called Gogmagog, who is associated with Plymouth Hoe. Later, in the 16th century, he was carved into the landscape there as two separate figures, Gog and Magog.

The oak trees depicted in the card were once part of an avenue of oaks which led a processional way towards Glastonbury Tor. It was used ceremonially by the Druids, and survived until 1906, when all but Gog and Magog were cut down to clear the land for a farm. One of the oak trees that did not survive was said to have 2,000 season rings, and was eleven feet in diameter.

Oak trees, and the mistletoe that grew on them, were sacred to the Druids. They were associated with fertility of the land and its inhabitants, and represented endurance, longevity, and triumph over obstacles. It is one of the miracles of nature that a tiny acorn can grow into a mighty oak tree that can live for thousands of years.

Gog and Magog are now protected under a conservation order. Within the trunk of Magog grows a new, tiny oak tree, a reminder of their ability for regeneration.

Gog and Magog rise majestically from the earth, their branches reaching out towards each other. Behind them, the sky graduates from a golden yellow, the colour of Leo, this card's astrological sign, to a clear blue. The Wheel Of Fortune, with its promise of change, moves us onward into this next stage of the journey, which brings the Strength to accept change joyfully, to immerse oneself in a lust for life.

The Strength card relates to the connection between the animalistic, instinctual nature and the rational, conscious mind. The instinctual nature needs to be understood, as it guides us through the subconscious mind, and creates patterns of behaviour that are difficult to change because they are deeply felt, and are not subject to reason. The Strength card shows us that we need to come to terms with the instinctual nature in order to understand what makes us who we are, and why we are drawn into certain patterns in our lives. We only need to tame it insofar as we are able to work with it constructively. The lion energy inherent in this card symbolises the dynamic force of the personality, which needs to be expressed in order for us to retain a sense of ourselves as an individual and a creative being.

Gog and Magog are fascinating trees to study. Faces and animals emerge from their trunks, creating a pantheon of otherworldly beings. Magog, on the left, shape-shifts into many different creatures on close observation. Several are shown in the image. There is a rearing lion, the symbol of this card, one of the most powerful and majestic of creatures. This shifts to become a boxing hare, representative of Goddess energy, and of Springtime, when the sap is rising and life is abundant with hope. A branch rises from her trunk like the horn of a unicorn, symbol of purity of action and intention; and smaller branches lean sideways like the antlers of a deer, a creature that represents gentleness. It is this state of trust in ourselves, and acceptance of the many facets of our inner nature, that the Strength card embodies.

The colours in the image are luminous. The trees are surrounded with golden light, indicative of the power of the mind and the ability to use this creatively, to find new solutions. The trees reflect the golden light within their trunks - the part of our body that holds us upright, that acts as a channel for our energy, and that enables us to carry our own weight and that of others. The deep brown of the shadows on the tree trunks indicate the earth qualities in ourselves, the ability to stay grounded in our sense of who we are. From Gog springs a grey branch, indicating the need to be able to be neutral, to look at all aspects of ourselves without judgement, with the knowledge that we need to fully express who and what we are.

DIVINATORY MEANING

The Strength card shows confidence, and the ability to deal with obstacles in a positive, even joyous, way. It indicates a phase of feeling passionate about your life, filled with hope for the future and the knowledge that you are strong enough to overcome anything that may stand in your way. Fears are swept aside, and so is any need for the approval of others.

This could be a time of great creativity for you, because you are now able to accept yourself as you are, and this enables you to give free rein to your energies. You are likely to feel supported and nurtured in your undertakings, because you are experiencing a deep sensitivity to your surroundings which enables you to make decisions consciously and with clarity.

THE HANGED MAN
THE FISHER KING

XII
THE HANGED MAN
THE FISHER KING

The image for this card is very different to many images of The Hanged Man. Its associations are with surrender, sacrifice, and patience, and usually the depiction is of a man hanging upside down from a tree, similar to the myth of Odin hanging from the World Tree. Yet the tale that gives rise to the image on this card is very appropriate to the overall meaning.

In card 0, The Fool, Percival stands on Wearyall Hill, gazing at a castle on the summit. This castle, called Corbenic, was home to the Fisher King. None knew how to find it, it was shrouded in mystery, and Percival stumbled upon it by accident. The Castle of Corbenic was home to a succession of guardians of the Holy Grail - the cup or chalice said to have been used for the sacrament at the Last Supper of Jesus and his disciples. Afterwards, Joseph Of Arimathea collected within it drops of blood from the Crucifixion, and brought it to Glastonbury. It passed on to the Castle of Corbenic, and was kept in the care of a succession of keepers said to be descended from Joseph.

One of these keepers was Percival's host, and another was the father of Elaine, who bore a son to Lancelot, called Galahad, who eventually became the knight who succeeded in attaining the Grail.

On Percival's arrival at the Castle, he was treated kindly. He noticed that the Fisher King had a wound in his groin that bled continually and refused to heal. The land around him was a wasteland, reflecting his bodily state. Having been taught that it was impolite to ask questions, Percival desisted, and pretended not to notice.

After the evening meal, a strange procession took place before them. Three maidens appeared, one bearing a lance that dripped blood, one bearing a sword, and the third carrying a chalice. Though curious, Percival watched in silence.

The following morning, Percival awoke to find that the castle and all its inhabitants had vanished. He went on his way, not realising that he had missed an opportunity to attain the Grail. The lance was the lance that had pierced the side of Christ at his crucifixion, and the chalice was the Holy Grail itself. If Percival had asked "What is the meaning of this?", or "Whom does the Grail serve?", the Fisher King and his land would have been healed, and Percival would have attained the Grail.

Years later, Percival was with Bors and Galahad when Galahad succeeded in the quest for the Grail.

THE IMAGE

The image shows the scene in the legend where the Grail procession is taking place. The Fisher King is seated on a throne covered in a green cloth, the colour of healing and balance. He wears a golden tunic and leggings, drawing on the healing energy of the sun, but his wound bleeds through these and down through the green cloth. He looks hopefully towards Percival, waiting for him to ask the question which will heal him and his land.

Percival stands beside him watching the procession with a look of amazement on his face. His white tunic and leggings reveal his innocence. He is pure and well-intentioned, but still too naive to realise the significance of what he is experiencing. In the background an ancient, ghostly figure is just visible through a doorway. He is the father of the Fisher King, rarely seen, sustained only by daily eating one communion wafer that has been placed in the Grail.

The castle walls are grey stone, giving a chill atmosphere. The woven carpet is a rich blue shade, denoting that there is an abundance of spiritual energy in this place, that this is an abode of high ideals requiring a measure of sacrifice.

The Fisher King card uses the instinctive drive of the Strength card to know when it is the right time for action, and when it is necessary to surrender the wants of the ego in order to support the needs of the higher Self.

DIVINATORY MEANING

The Hanged Man shows a state of inner peace that enables us to accept even difficult situations, with the patience that comes from knowing that there is a right time for everything, and to try to force a solution to an issue would not be beneficial.

The card teaches us that what we need will come to us in due course, and that, at the moment, an attitude of surrender and patience is necessary. A push for change at this time would only create more obstacles. The ego sees surrender as a kind of death, yet it really reflects an awareness that life has its own rhythms, and there is a time to move forward and a time to stand still and reflect on what our present situation has to teach us. The Hanged Man can signify that you have been experiencing great difficulty in your life, and that now is the time to let go, to listen to your inner self. Through the increased awareness of listening to your intuition, a reversal of your situation can occur.

There is a great sense of inner peace present in this card. The father of the Fisher King is able to survive with very little sustenance, showing that we do not always need all that we think we need, and that we are being looked after by a force that we may not understand, but which functions nevertheless. The Fisher King hopes for the situation to change, but he is also aware that if Percival does not ask the question, someone else will.

In a reading, this card reminds you that you need to pause before acting; to evaluate the facts of your situation, and wait for the right solution to present itself.

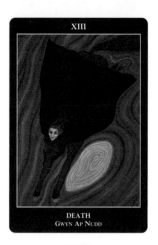

XIII

XIII
DEATH
GWYN AP NUDD

The Faery-Folk encompassed a wide variety of beings of all shapes and sizes, from the small elves and gnomes to the tall, dark beings that were associated with Gwyn Ap Nudd - King of the Faeries and Lord of the Underworld. They could be kind and benevolent, mischievous, and some were downright malevolent. Certainly they were untrustworthy, and were viewed by the populace with a degree of fear and suspicion, although mortals went to great lengths to propitiate them.

The Faeries made their homes in hollow hills, and lived outside of mortal time. Mortals straying into, or invited into their domain could remain there for years, thinking only days had passed. It was unwise to partake of the food or drink of the Faeries, as this could make you their prisoner - a fact that St. Collen was well aware of when Gwyn Ap Nudd invited him to a feast. (See Card IX. The Hermit).

Gwyn Ap Nudd lived with his subjects in the hollow hill of Glastonbury Tor. He was considered to be diabolic by the early Christians, who viewed the Pagan and Faery ways as demonic. One legend says that the maze or labyrinth on Glastonbury Tor was a faery path. The first Christian church built on top of the Tor, dedicated to St. Michael, collapsed in 1275 - apparently due to an earthquake, but more widely believed to have been caused by the influence of Gwyn and his subjects.

Card VI, The Lovers, relates the tale of Gwyn Ap Nudd's abduction of Creiddylad; and Card IX, The Hermit, describes how St. Collen banished Gwyn from the top of the Tor. The influence of the King of the Faeries is still felt in Glastonbury, but Gwyn Ap Nudd also had another title - Lord of the Underworld. In this guise, he rode on his pale horse through the skies at Winter Solstice to gather in the souls of the dead, accompanied by the hounds of Annwn, white dogs with red ears. He then took the souls back to the Underworld to prepare them for the next stage of their journey.

THE IMAGE

Gwyn Ap Nudd rides across the sky to gather in the souls of the dead. Under the light of the moon and stars, his skin and black hair have a blue sheen. The sky below him swirls with energy, in shades of blue and purple. Far below is Glastonbury Tor, distinguishable by its labyrinth, which glows white in the light of the moon and stars.

His horse looks fierce. Its eyes glow red, its teeth are bared as it propels itself through the sky. Gwyn uses no reins or saddle - he clings to the horse's neck, revelling in the chase. Purple is sometimes associated with death, as it represents a change to a new, and higher, state of consciousness.

Gwyn Ap Nudd's black cloak flies behind him, as if it would spread out to darken the entire sky. Black is the symbol of the void, the state of emptiness wherein lie the seeds of potential waiting to take form.

DIVINATORY MEANING

The Death card signifies an ending that leads us to a new beginning. It indicates a time to let go of the past. It can denote the ending of a phase of life, a job, or a relationship because the situation has run its course; all that can be learned from it has been integrated, and it is time to move on, to seek new areas of experience in the arena of life. This card does not indicate physical death; its influence paves the way for a fresh beginning in your life, and shows that letting go of attachments can be painful but are ultimately rewarding.

The lesson of the Hanged Man card is surrender, of undergoing a transition period when there is a need to wait for events to run their course. The Death card moves us onwards into action; it encourages us to push for change, to put behind us all of the factors which have held us back, to sever connections that are no longer helpful to us and do not support us. In order to do this, we need to recognise any fears of change that can hinder us from moving into a new beginning.

The Death card is the card of cleansing, allowing us to experience the transformation of our circumstances just as the caterpillar that willingly, even joyfully, becomes a butterfly.

XIV
TEMPERANCE
BRIGIT

St. Brigit followed in the footsteps of St. Patrick, from her native Ireland to Glastonbury. She lived at the Beckery, a convent which later was the scene of a mystical vision experienced by King Arthur. His vision of the Virgin and Child was so powerful that Arthur was converted to Christianity, and wore an emblem of them on his shield. A copy of this can still be seen at the entrance to the ruins of Glastonbury Abbey.

Bride's Mound, an area of land near the Beckery, is dedicated to St. Brigit, and also to the Goddess Bride or Bridie, with whom Brigit is associated. Brigit was reputed to have spent a great deal of time at Bride's Mound. A chapel was dedicated to her, which emanated healing energy. All who passed through a special opening in the chapel were healed of their ills. Bride's Mound has long been neglected, and overgrown by nettles, though a Glastonbury group named "Friends Of Bride's Mound" has been campaigning to restore this sacred place to its former beauty. The area is home to many creatures, and deer will wander close if you are quiet and watch for them.

THE IMAGE

St. Brigit stands at the bottom of Chalice Hill. Her hair glows red-gold in the subtle light filtering through the trees. It is the colour of flame, and reflects her association with the Goddess Bridie, patron of fire, of the forge, of holy wells, and of healing. Her dress is the deep blue of devotion to a spiritual ideal, and flows to her ankles, revealing her bare feet which shows that although her commitment is to the spirit, she retains a relationship with the earth and is able to anchor her energy and use it for the good of others.

She stands with one foot in the water, and the other on dry land. Her posture shows that she is in a state of perfect balance. Two water-lilies float before her; flowers that, like the lotus, gain nutrients from the mud, float in the water, and open their blossoms into the air. These are symbols of our ability to exist at all levels of our being - to open ourselves to the spiritual aspects of ourselves while remaining rooted in the earth that sustains our physical form.

In her hands, Brigit holds two chalices. The elements of earth, air, fire and water flow from each, merging so that they are not poured onto the ground, but instead create an alchemical force that flows in both directions from chalice to chalice. With these, Brigit harnesses the powerful forces of nature and creates a union of opposites. There is great creative energy in this, as the blending of opposing factors acts as a force for change and transformation. This gives rise to a new and beautiful energy, which is brought forth from deep within the self.

A thorn tree leans towards Brigit, its branches festooned with ribbons, a descendant of a thorn tree that once overlooked Bride's Well. Some call these "wishing trees", for you can make a wish while tying a ribbon upon a branch, and can tie another ribbon on it later in order to give thanks if a wish has been granted. Outside the White Spring at Wellhouse Lane, Glastonbury, there is another tree that has been decorated in this fashion.

DIVINATORY MEANING

After the fulfilment of the need for a new beginning signified by the Death card, comes the urge to seek and create balance within yourself. This card shows there is a need to explore dimensions of your inner self, to discover what you feel is important to you. The focus of this card is that of balance - the equilibrium that results from the knowledge that we are many-faceted beings, and can develop any aspects of ourselves that we wish to.

The meaning of Temperance is balance and moderation. Extremes should be avoided; it is important at this time of new discovery of the creative aspects of yourself that you keep your centre and don't go rushing off at a tangent. Changes are taking place within you, so give them time to make themselves felt. A sense of inner peace is engendered by this card, a feeling that hitherto unrecognised aspects of yourself are providing a recognition of your inner strength.

XV
THE DEVIL
ST. DUNSTAN

St. Dunstan was born in Baltonsborough, near Glastonbury, in 909 CE. He was of noble ancestry, related by birth to the ruling house of Wessex, and grew up to become a remarkable man, renowned for his intelligence, culture, creative and musical skills, as well as visionary qualities.

Dunstan was educated at Glastonbury Abbey, and dreamed of making it a great landmark to Christianity and culture. Yet he was also very broad-minded, and curious about other philosophies and ways of life. He possessed great physical beauty, and attracted much attention from women.

In those days, the King's Court was often held at Cheddar, in Somerset. When Dunstan's education was completed, he became a courtier there. His charm and good looks endeared him to the women there, and there was talk of a marriage between him and one of the Ladies. The male courtiers viewed him with a great deal of jealousy, and plotted against him. Dunstan's interest in religions other than Christianity was their cue to have him banished from court on suspicion of heresy. He left under a cloud, and on his way home to Glastonbury was set upon, beaten, and left for dead in a bog - the Germanic punishment for crimes against morality.

However, he survived, and made his weary way to Glastonbury Abbey.

There he became a monk , and lived at the Abbey. In his leisure hours he built a forge, created beautiful works of art, and explored his musical talents. Strange phenomena were observed to take place around him, including huge pieces of masonry inexplicably falling to the ground at his feet.

When King Edmund acceeded to the throne, Dunstan was recalled to court to act as his advisor. Again, he became a focal point for the envy of the male courtiers, but Edmund favoured him. He made Dunstan the Abbot of Glastonbury, and Dunstan fulfilled his youthful vision by extending the original buildings and adding side chapels and a tower. He also ensured that the everyday work of the Abbey inhabitants was made efficient and productive. Dunstan's vision made the Abbey a place of renown that lived on long after his death.

In 956 CE, Dunstan was made Archbishop, and acted as virtual Regent to the new child-king, Edgar. He presided over his coronation, and after Edgar's untimely death, went on to crown Athelred. His wisdom and kindliness were known across the land.

The final phase of Dunstan's life was spent in contemplation and prayer, and his leisure time was taken up in the making of musical instruments. In May 988 he preached his last sermon, and died on the 19th of May. The night before his death is still known as St. Dunstan's Eve. He was recognised as a saint almost immediately after his death, and was buried at Glastonbury Abbey.

During his life, Dunstan had many visions. Some reports say that he was epileptic; certainly he had periods of ill-health and depression. There are stories that Dunstan had visions of the devil trying to tempt him, and he would chase the devil away with red-hot tongs from his forge. Although celibate, he had several close friendships with women, and others attempted unsuccessfully to seduce him.

In one famous tale, the devil came to Dunstan in the form of a beautiful temptress. Dunstan saw through the disguise, and, spotting a hoof peeping out from beneath her, took his tongs from the forge and pinched the devil's nose. The devil ran off screaming, and jumped into the river.

THE IMAGE

St. Dunstan stands ready for attack, brandishing his red-hot tongs, as a naked woman reaches out towards him. His face is a mask of horror and outrage as he steps back towards the flames belching from his forge, then lunges to attack. His monk's robes are brown, signifying the renunciation of ways of the flesh, and the practical application of his spiritual insights.

The woman smiles seductively at him, certain of her power to draw him towards her. She cups her breast in her right hand, offering herself to him, and reaches out to draw him close with her left hand. Her hair, which in those days was worn bound by respectable women, hangs loose and flows down her back.

Behind them, a great spiral of energy emerges, ready to suck them into its vortex. A pair of demonic eyes glare out, and a huge scarlet clawed hand, its nails black with malice, looms towards them. Behind the figure of Dunstan, flames shoot from his forge, threatening to engulf him.

DIVINATORY MEANING

The state of balance brought about through XIV, Temperance, allows all aspects of the Self to be recognised, weighed and measured. In the quest for self-knowledge, nothing in the psyche is left hidden, and all the dark corners of the mind are illuminated by the emerging rays of the light of self-understanding.

The Devil card represents all the fears we have suppressed, coming to the surface so that they can be swept away and dissolved into the light. Another aspect of this card is temptation. Are you strong enough to resist it? The temptations denoted by this card are not real; they are illusory, there to make you think about what you truly want, and which path is the right one to follow.

This card is about the power of desire, and the need to see the material world as merely a necessary aspect of the spiritual - to be able to enjoy it without being caught up in the illusion that the physical is all that exists. The Devil shows us our fears, our desires and our obsessions, and teaches us that if we are true to ourselves, we cannot be bound by them.

In a reading, The Devil card indicates the need to face our fears in order to conquer them. It can reveal an attraction to someone who is not suitable or truly compatible, based on the sexual element only. You may be facing up to a feeling of depression, or of feeling bound by a person or situation. Now is the time to realise that you have the power to change this, through an act of will.

The Devil card has links with the Pagan nature god, Pan. His energy is bawdy, lustful, vital, creative and mischievous. The word 'panic' stems from his name - the feeling of losing control, because the ecstasy generated by his energetic presence can be too much to assimilate. The Devil reminds you not to take yourself too seriously; to allow yourself to have some fun, but with an awareness of what you really want to attract into your life.

XVI
THE TOWER
THE TOR

Glastonbury Tor is a 500 foot high conical hill, topped by the ruins of a church dedicated to St. Michael. In olden days, the land around the Tor was surrounded by water. Glastonbury was an island, linked with Avalon, and viewed with fear and reverence by early Christians because of its Pagan associations. The views from the top of the Tor are breathtakingly beautiful, and extend for miles. In times of flood, it is possible to climb the Tor and see how it must have looked untold years ago.

The Tor has always retained an aura of mystery. Pilgrims from all the different faiths gather here to marvel at the landscape and the ruins of the church, to observe religious rites, and to absorb the mystical energies of Glastonbury and Avalon.

It seems as if the Tor has always been here, as old as time itself. It was used by ancient peoples as a site of worship, probably to the Goddess. Druids came to the Tor, then Christians settled here. The spiral maze or labyrinth cut into the sides of the Tor is extremely ancient, carved carefully by hand for ceremonial purposes. Graves have been found here, and artifacts left by the Picts, Celts and Romans.

Links between the Tor and the Underworld and Otherworld are

strong even now. It is said to be the home of Gwyn Ap Nudd, King of the Faeries and Lord of the Underworld, who lives in the hollow beneath the Tor. (See Card VI, The Lovers, Card IX, The Hermit, and Card XIII, Death). There are caves here, and tunnels were discovered, one leading from the Abbey to the Tor. These were blocked up after excavators went in to investigate. Some never returned, others came back crazy, or dumb, unable to explain what they had found.

Dowsers have ascertained that the Tor is certainly hollow, and that it houses underground springs, and possibly an internal version of the spiral maze. Visitors to the Tor often experience an otherworldly feeling, a loss of their sense of time, and sometimes mystical visions. The Tor still has the power to enchant and enrapture. Walking the spiral maze to and from the top of the Tor in a ceremonial fashion is seen as a form of initiation, leading to an increased sense of empowerment and a symbolic rebirth.

THE IMAGE

The Tor rises above the landscape, out of reach of the lashing waves of flood-water that attempt, and fail, to engulf it. The spiral maze casts shadows on the sides of the earth mound, and the top of the Tor reflects the light cast by a rising phoenix - symbol of death and rebirth. The tower of the ruined St. Michael's church stands out darkly, illuminated within by a flame that sears the breast of the phoenix.

The phoenix flaps its wings as it rises above the Tor, casting feathers of flame out into the night sky. The flame within its breast represents the flame at the heart of man/woman, the indestructible life-force, the power of the heart to consume grief and fear and still survive. The mythical phoenix is said to cast itself into the flames of destruction at the apparent end of its life, to lay an egg within those flames before it perishes, then to be reborn from that egg, and rise anew.

The flood-water is the tide of emotion that, if unchecked by the grounded element of ourselves, represented by the Tor, can threaten to overwhelm us and cause us to lose control.

The image of The Tower is the image of destruction in order to create anew. The phoenix brings with it a promise of rebirth, a sense of the calm after the storm.

DIVINATORY MEANING

If we have not taken note of the lessons of The Devil card, and are unable to break away from our fears and habit patterns, The Tower accomplishes this for us. It brings a time of upheaval, when the fire of purification burns away the dross in our lives, leaving us possibly exhausted, but certainly clear-headed.

The Tower is the great awakener. It tears away the veils that prevent us from seeing things clearly, and this can be painful because sometimes it is easier to hold onto our illusions than face a difficult truth. Yet face it we must - The Tower gives us no other choice. This process is one of transformation at a very deep level, and makes the space in our life for a new form of energy and experience. There is no other way to deal with your current situation than to let go, to allow it to happen, to experience what you are experiencing without fighting or denying it. The only action to take is to wait for the storm to blow over - and it will. You may feel as though you have been washed up on a foreign shore with no map, but this is actually a time when you can experience yourself as a strong, empowered being, programmed for survival.

The Tower can also signify a sudden flash of insight, a realisation that can bring forth a state of ecstasy and which can change your life in an instant - the inexplicable feeling of Eureka! that has given rise to some of the most important scientific discoveries. But this discovery is about yourself, about who and what you are. The gifts of The Tower, though they can seem harsh, open the way to a powerful, true sense of Self.

XVII
THE STAR
BRIDE'S MOUND

Bride's Mound is a small, rounded hill, sacred to the Goddess Bridie - patroness of fire, creativity, childbirth and healing. Bridie, also known as Brigit, Brighid, and Brid, was a Celtic Goddess revered by blacksmiths, poets, doctors and priests. She was a Goddess of sovereignty - representing the spouse of the King of the land who ensures the prosperity and fertility of the kingdom.

Bridie's Day is Imbolc, 1st February, the first day of spring. In Glastonbury the tradition still remains of making a Bridie doll each Imbolc, to bring fertility to the land.

St. Brigit is seen as the personification of the Goddess Bridie, (See XIV, Temperance). She was born near Kildare, Ireland, was baptised as a nun by St. Patrick, and founded a monastery at Kildare. She later followed St. Patrick to Glastonbury, and lived in a convent at the Beckery, close to Bride's Mound. Like her namesake, Bridie, she was associated with the qualities of love and compassion, and was called upon in prayer by blacksmiths, healers, craftspeople and poets. She died in 525 CE.

Bride's mound is dedicated to Bridie and to St. Brigit. It was reputed to be a place of healing, and, as with all places sacred to Bridie, had a healing well, overlooked by a thorn tree, hung with ribbons and gifts to the Goddess and Saint. It dried up long ago, and its site is now marked by a headstone. This is where the mysterious Blue Bowl (see Ace Of Chalices) was discovered.

The Mound, sadly, is now overgrown, and has to be looked for beneath the nettles that flourish there. But its atmosphere is still magical - there is a great stillness at this site, a sense of sanctity, and wild creatures sense this and come here. The view from Bride's Mound, if you ignore the intrusion of sewage works, is a spectacular vista encompassing Chalice Hill and Wearyall Hill, backed by Glastonbury Tor.

THE IMAGE

Bride's Mound shines green in the starlight - the colour of healing, of balance, and of creativity. The trees around the Mound seem to create the effect of a magic circle.

Behind Bride's Mound rise the slopes of Chalice Hill on the left, Wearyall Hill on the right, and the Tor in the centre. It is a magical view, a vision of four sacred sites, all imbued with the qualities of mystery, healing and peaceful repose. If you look at the image with a relaxed eye, it can seem like the body of a reclining woman - the Goddess of the land. The Tor and Wearyall Hill could be her breasts, topped by the nipples of the tower on the Tor and the trees at the summit of Wearyall Hill. Chalice Hill could be her belly, and Bride's Mound her womb, her centre of gravity and fertility.

In the sky above them shines the Bear, or Plough, constellation. The Bear is sacred to King Arthur, whose Roman name, Arturus, means Bear. This reveals the great strength which we all carry within ourselves, and the ability to go within, to be introspective in order to know ourselves, which enables us to then have more understanding of others. Bears can be fierce, but they are also gentle with their cubs, and they represent the harnessing of great powers of inner strength.

DIVINATORY MEANING

After the shattered illusions of The Tower, and the insights into our true nature, come the peace and hope for the future engendered by The Star. All feels well with the world. We have passed through the eye of the storm and have now emerged intact. Life glows with promise and possibilities, the crisis has passed, and there is now a sense of glorious freedom, of new and vibrant energy. We are able to connect with the conscious mind as well as the unconscious, and realise that we have the ability to bring our dreams to fruition.

The Star in a reading signifies a blissful state of inner peace, a feeling of benevolence towards the world and ourselves. This is a time of hope, of renewal, and of healing. You can now be who you truly are, and can trust in the power of your intuition, your inner knowing. This clarity of vision brings a new purpose to your life, and that enables people to be drawn to you who can help you fulfil that purpose.

Now is the time to dream your dreams, to bring them into form, because your confidence in yourself is blossoming. You feel connected to yourself and to the rest of the world, and your trust in the ability of the universe to fulfil your needs will be borne out by the opportunities which will now present themselves to you.

THE MOON
CHALICE HILL

XVIII
THE MOON
CHALICE HILL

Chalice Hill is a beautiful rounded hill close to the Tor. The atmosphere there is soft and feminine, peaceful and tranquil. It takes its name from the Chalice, the Holy Grail that is so powerfully linked with the legends of Jesus and King Arthur, and has as its roots the Cauldron of Inspiration and Plenty sacred to the Celts. Chalice Hill provides a sanctuary, a refuge from the cares of everyday life.

After the death of Arthur, Bedivere was said to have lived in a hermitage on its southern slopes, joined after Guinevere's death by Lancelot and other Knights of the Round Table. The site of the hermitage is thought to be where Chalice Well is now situated. The Grail, or Cauldron, was reputed to represent the heart energy - that which gives unconditional love to all who come to it. Legends say that the Grail was buried within Chalice Hill. Sitting on its gentle slopes, listening to the birdsong and the wind whispering through the trees, it is easy to believe in the ancient myths, and to feel their presence still.

Rising from the slopes of the hill is a grove of Ash trees, and near them a huge, ancient Lime tree spreads its roots and branches majestically into the earth and sky. Cows meander there, curiously watching the pilgrims who come seeking the tranquillity of the landscape in order to find it within themselves. The Lime tree has hollows and caves within its roots, and moss grows on its trunk, which shines luminous and mysterious in the light of the moon.

THE IMAGE

The Lime tree stands alone on the upper slopes of Chalice Hill. Behind it, the full moon rises, casting light on the mossy trunk and throwing the branches into dark relief. The Lime, or Linden tree as it is also called, is symbolic of protection. Having a Lime tree in your garden, or placing Lime branches outside your door, brings protection to the occupants. Its leaves and flowers can be drunk as a tea, or dried and placed in a pouch, to bring love to the imbiber or wearer.

Dried Lime blossom or leaves, infused in hot water, aid restful sleep, and are cures for insomnia; pillows can also be made for that purpose with a mixture of Lime and Lavender flowers. The wood, if carried, can bring the wearer good fortune - aided by the tree's relationship with Jupiter, the planet of expansion, luck, sociability, and study.

In the image, the moon is full. Often, a dark moon is associated with this card, symbolising a time to go deep within yourself, to face the dark guardians who stand at the threshold, or gateway, to deep spiritual knowledge; and to gather the courage to step forward across that threshold into a new and powerful dimension of inner knowing. Once experienced, the dark moon waxes to become the full moon, the blossoming that can now take place of the seeds you have planted - just as the dark soil nourishes and nurtures the seeds of plants until they are strong enough to push upwards into the light.

The Moon is associated with cycles of waxing and waning within nature and within ourselves. Its movement governs the tides of water that cover the earth, and that reside within our cells. The moon's pull is subtle, but extremely powerful. It rules the unconscious mind and the subconscious - those aspects of ourselves which remain hidden, yet influence our every action, until we choose to plumb those depths and bring its treasures to the surface.

The qualities associated with the moon are those of intuition, of inner knowing, of mystery, of the feminine and her ability to reproduce. It rules the realm of the imagination, where hopes and fears can be distorted, or moulded into a blueprint for the future. The Moon reflects light - it reveals the mystery that lies behind all outward things. The word lunacy stems from the moon, and it is well documented that the full moon has a disturbing effect upon those who are sensitive.

The Moon also gives us the courage to fulfil our dreams and potential. The emotions can be channelled into a mighty force that focuses us on the tides within ourselves which can be harnessed and used for our benefit. The most successful people are those who feel passionately about their lives and work, and who are able to tap into their inner power, use their emotions as a guide, and listen to their 'gut feelings' as well as their logical mind.

DIVINATORY MEANING

The inner peace, and the feelings of hope engendered by The Star take us within ourselves. The Star, like the Sun, gives off light of its own. The Moon reflects light, and reminds us that all is not always as it seems. It teaches us to plough deep into the furrows, to seek out the seeds of truth, while enabling the imagination and the creative faculties of the mind to come into full play.

In a reading, The Moon symbolises a time of deep insight and understanding, a time to listen to what your inner self is telling you, and to courageously dispel your fears by facing them. It signals that your intuition is strong, and should be listened to.

The Moon symbolises an awakening of your psychic abilities, an opening of the gates to deeper understanding that will lead to new experience. This is a time of magic, when you can accomplish much by truly listening to your inner needs, and allowing your creative instincts to work for you. The Moon can also signify deception, so it is important that you remain true to yourself, and take notice of the feelings that you pick up from the people around you.

The action of The Tower is to tear away the veil of illusion that prevents you from clear sight. The Moon offers you the opportunity to draw aside the veil that covers the gateway to inner vision. By doing this, you are able to step into a deep sense of connection between yourself and all things, based on an inner knowing that resides, through feeling, at the cellular level.

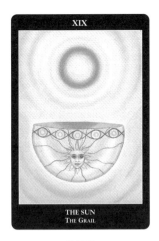

XIX
THE SUN
THE GRAIL

The Grail is the Holy Grail, the chalice used by Christ at the Last Supper, and afterwards by his uncle, Joseph of Arimathea, who collected within it drops of blood from Christ's crucifixion. It is also the Cauldron of Nourishment sacred to the Celts, the Cauldron of Plenty that provided all with an abundance of the foods of their choice.

The Hanged Man card tells the story of the Fisher King, waiting for Percival to ask the vital question "Whom does the Grail serve?" The wound in the groin of the Fisher King was reflected in the barrenness of his land, and indicates that the wound was sexual in nature, related to fertility and fecundity - attributes of The Sun. The Fisher King's ancient father was sustained through eating only one communion wafer daily, which had been placed in the Grail, indicating that the Grail is a fount of life, whose healing magic is allowed to flow freely once the right magic words are uttered.

One of the Arthurian legends describes how this ancient father entered Annwn, the land of Gwyn Ap Nudd, to steal the Cauldron of Inspiration and Plenty. The Castle of Corbenic, home of the Fisher King, was said to be at Wearyall Hill, and the Grail Castle itself was situated on the Tor, the abode of Gwyn Ap Nudd. This hints that the treasures of the soul, of union with the spiritual aspects of the Self and with the creative Force that brings all things into being, is attained through knowledge of the Underworld, of the hidden elements in our nature. This knowledge is experienced through The Moon card, and brought out into the light of The Sun card, which enables us to express those qualities openly and freely.

The quest for the Grail is the search for enlightenment - which, once attained, brings the realisation that this exalted state has always been here within us, waiting only to be discovered. The Grail quest undertaken by King Arthur's Knights is the quest for the knowledge of the immortality of the soul. Once attained, there is no need for a physical expression of it, as a Chalice, because that is merely a symbol created to inspire us on our journey towards the discovery of that state. The tarot is a map for that journey, and is also a guide which leads us onward through the realms of inner and outer experiences, to discover the core of our true selves.

THE IMAGE

The Sun shines brightly, filling the card with dazzling golden light. Its energy spins outwards, from the white core glowing at its centre, to a deep orange, the colour of positivity and action, at its edges. Muted colours spiral in shifting bands of yellow (the conscious mind, clarity, happiness), to white, (purity of thought and action, and the activation of a state of potential), to pink, which shows the unconditional love of Creator for Creation.

Floating in bands of golden light is the Grail, the Holy Chalice, merging with the energy of the sun, and at the same time, reflecting it. Jewels are studded like eyes at the rim of the Grail, reflecting so much light that their nature cannot be identified. The surround continues the appearance of many eyes - the eyes of the spirit, which see and accept all.

A face emerges from the Grail, an image of the Goddess of sovereignty - she who takes care of all life, and gives it nourishment. From her emerge many small flames, radiating from her luminous skin - the flames of the many facets of her, and our, being. A single large flame burns brightly above her forehead, representing the indestructible flame of the spirit, of higher knowledge, of intuition, and of union with the Divine.

Light crackles across the Grail, emanating from the Goddess - the light of life that manifests itself through everything in existence. The

sun shines on all beings, sentient and insentient, with no discrimi-
nation and no need for reciprocation. It merely is content to be
itself. The sun can burn, wither away, or heal, warm, purify and
inspire, and it is our choice as to how we expose ourselves to its
light. The light of the sun illuminates all aspects of ourselves, casts
shadows with its passing, can be obscured by clouds of negative
thoughts - yet it is always there.

DIVINATORY MEANING

The Sun represents knowledge. In its journey across the sky, it sees
all, and accepts it with an unbiased eye. It signifies joy, positivity,
growth and union. Its rulership of the astrological sign Leo brings
expansion, the manifestation of creativity, and an overwhelming
love of life.

In a reading, The Sun reminds you to recognise the beauty all
around you. You are moving into a time of great happiness and
success, and this is likely to be reflected in beneficial opportunities
to expand your creativity and your sense of harmony with those
around you. This brings success in areas of love, relationships, and
career opportunities. Your confidence will increase as you receive
positive feedback and support from others, and you are able to
accomplish a great deal.

This is the card of optimism, high energy, and an all-pervading
sense of unity. You are now able to fulfil the wishes and desires that
have been germinating through the energies of The Star and The
Moon cards, and the world looks bright with promise.

XX
JUDGEMENT
ST. MICHAEL

On top of Glastonbury Tor stands a ruined church, dedicated to St. Michael, the Archangel. It is situated on the Michael line, and is part of a long alignment of sacred monuments and churches that stretches in a straight line across southern England, from Land's End in Cornwall, to East Anglia. These sites are built, or are natural landmarks, on hill tops, marking a pathway of light across the land. Hilltops were dedicated to St. Michael because, as Archangel, Michael is the mediator between heaven and earth.

St. Michael was the Light-Bringer, whose flaming sword banished evil and defeated the powers of darkness. The Michael Line is an alignment of leys. Leys or ley lines are channels for earth energy, similar to the meridians in our bodies that acupuncturists treat when practising healing, and another name for them is dragon-paths.

Christian mythology describes St. Michael as slaying the dragon of Paganism, whereas the temples built to him on the hilltops that his ley line passes through are dedicated to controlling the dragon-energy that flows through the earth, promulgating a healing energy.

THE IMAGE

St. Michael hovers above the top of the Tor, his robe merging with the sky, the blue of spiritual devotion and clarity of thought. His wings and hair are golden, radiating light, reflecting the colours of the pure, spiritual energy of the sun, that illuminates all things.

In his hands, he clasps the sword of insight, cool at its centre but surrounded by flames which have the power to purify all that they touch. His face is serene, and he gazes outwards in a manner which indicates benevolence but also detachment. Light from his sword spreads out into the surrounding sky, which bears no hint of clouds. He is the all-wise, all-seeing one, who is able to act without allowing his emotions to interfere.

DIVINATORY MEANING

Judgement represents the call to a more meaningful way of life. The Sun card dispelled all illusions, showed us that we are surrounded by great beauty and harmony, and allowed us to remove the final barriers to clear vision of who and what we are. Judgement calls us to look for the meaning in every aspect of our existence. It gives us a pure and elevated overview of our situation - the ability to soar like an eagle and see things from a new perspective. It is a process of witnessing the death of the ego, the part of ourselves that wants to keep us small, and the rebirth of the wisdom aspects and the spiritual Self. Judgement teaches us the meaning of our existence, and causes us to question, and to find answers to why we are here.

In a reading, Judgement shows that this is the time to push for change, to leave behind the old ways that no longer serve you, and to move towards the new, with an increased awareness of yourself. Changes have already taken place within you, and you can now allow yourself to joyously enter a new phase of your life.

This card represents the ability to analyse, to discriminate, and to act on insights you have gained, so that you can move towards that which supports you, and leave behind that which hinders you. You can now experience an increased sense of clarity, which will inspire you to move forward with joy and confidence.

XXI
THE WORLD
THE PHOENIX

The World card is the culmination of the journey begun by card 0, The Fool. The path has been followed through all its stages of inner and outer transformation, and the end of this leads us to a new beginning. Life moves in spirals, not circles, and there is always somewhere further to go. Even the state of liberation and enlightenment signified by The World is but the first step on a new journey of discovery.

The centre of existence is everywhere, within everything. The mirror depicted in The World card represents the 0 of The Fool. The contours of the Tor and labyrinth follow the colours of the rainbow, the journey of initiation through all aspects and experiences of life. The experience of The World card is the knowledge that the state of completion it embodies is reflected in everything else. We are able to feel ourselves to be an integral part of the whole, shifting and merging to encompass many new dimensions and ways of being.

The egg-stone depicted in the image is a symbol of wholeness, and of the seed, the beginning. There is an egg-stone in Glastonbury Abbey. The egg-stone represents the Omphalos - the centre of the world, and the source of life itself.

The phoenix is a symbol of rebirth, and also features in card XVI,

The Tower. It signifies the emergence of ourselves from the purifying flames of St. Michael's sword in the Judgement card, to rise again with an ecstatic awareness of our true nature.

THE IMAGE

The World card shows a beautiful, abstract phoenix rising. Her feathers shimmer, yet are unruffled by her experiences of rebirth. From her body emerges the egg-stone, radiating opalescent light. The green area near its centre symbolises healing, harmony, creativity and balance, and is situated at the point where a hole passes through the egg-stone. This represents the journey into a new dimension of life - in a similar fashion to the theory in quantum physics that black holes in space are portals to parallel universes. The World card shows that we can experience that transformation in the here and now, and create our own universe out of our insights and wisdom.

The phoenix clasps within her wings a circular mirror, the Mirror of the Self which, when gazed into, shows your true face - Buddhists call it your "original" face. To look into the magic mirror and experience your true self is to experience liberation from all bondage and longings, because all that you could wish for in life is present in the here and now.

The face of the phoenix is totally peaceful and benign. She has united within herself the male and female elements, and she gazes knowingly at you, for she sees your true nature, and loves and accepts you because she also recognises herself in you. On her forehead is the spiral of rebirth, which is also like a seed of new beginnings.

Below the phoenix is the Tor, its labyrinth rainbow-hued, a symbol of the integration of all your life experiences. The purpose of the labyrinth is initiatory; it is the enactment of the journey to the centre of yourself, then back again into the world, bringing the wisdom you have gained in order to use it in your everyday life.

Behind the phoenix, a deep blue night sky opens out, studded with tiny stars, symbolising the new world that is opening up to you now that all tests and challenges have been met and overcome. The stars promise the fulfilment of your potential and your dreams.

Bordering the image are the colours of the elements. The yellow-brown on the left is earth; light green is air; scarlet is fire; and blue is water. They relate also to the four cardinal directions of north, east, south and west. These signify that you are now able to recognise, balance, and use all these elements within yourself. You can remain grounded (yellow-brown), while you understand (green), in order to be inspired (red) and act on your deepest feelings (blue) - and this can then be manifested through re-entering the earth energy in order to bring into being what you have created. The spiral is ongoing, and eternal.

DIVINATORY MEANING

The World card denotes a deep understanding of yourself, and a feeling of being at peace with yourself and at one with the universe. It is the state of ecstasy and unity that comes from a feeling of completeness and completion. It symbolises the accomplishment of a task that leaves you with a feeling of liberation. You are able to see everything as it truly is; all the masks have dropped away and you are able to look around you in astonishment that life can be so good!

All negativity around you has been dissolved. You are going in the direction that is right for you, that will bring harmony and success because no blockages are strong enough to stand in your way. Your positivity and confidence can over-ride anything, because you know what is truly right for you.

A new and beautiful phase in your life is beginning. Each step you have taken has led you to this. Now is the time to move forwards with a dance in your step, and your hands open wide to accept the gifts of the universe.

THE MINOR ARCANA

ACE OF STAFFS
THE GLASTONBURY THORN

ACE OF STAFFS
THE GLASTONBURY THORN

The Ace of Staffs is represented by the Glastonbury Thorn tree, which derives from a staff planted in the earth on Wearyall Hill by Joseph of Arimathea, almost 2,000 years ago. The thorn tree that can be seen now at the same spot as the original tree is one of its descendants, and grew from a cutting. Another descendant of the same tree can be seen in the grounds of St. John's church, Glastonbury, and a cutting of its blossom is sent to the Queen each Christmas when it flowers.

THE IMAGE

The Ace of Staffs, the Glastonbury Thorn tree, rises from the earth emanating vigour and radiating a powerful life-force. Below the tree is a circle of light, representing the seed of new life which contains within it all potential for growth. The grass around the base of the tree is inlaid with a spiral design, indicating that life moves in spirals, and that endings lead to new beginnings - just as the original thorn tree has lived on through cuttings taken from it and its descendants.

The tree is surrounded by light that blazes from it and radiates out into the surrounding land. It is a symbol of new and vibrant life, of energy that cannot be contained but must permeate its surroundings.

DIVINATORY MEANING

The Ace of Staffs symbolises new and exciting beginnings. It is a seed card, indicating that the energy is now available for you to accomplish whatever you set out to do. This is the highest energy card in the tarot pack, apart from The Sun, and The King of Staffs, and shows you that all blockages to your success have now been removed, and you can move swiftly forward with confidence.

The Ace of Staffs signifies a time of renewal, and of transformation. New opportunities are about to be offered filling you with a sense of optimism and eagerness. You now have the inner strength to step forward and put your ideas into action, with the knowledge that success is awaiting you.

2 OF STAFFS
GATEWAY

2 OF STAFFS
GATEWAY

THE IMAGE

A man stands at the top of Wearyall Hill, holding aloft two staffs entwined with snakes, symbols of the regenerative energy and the wisdom aspect of ourselves. His feet are obscured by the long grass - he is grounded in his vision of what he wants from life, and what he has to offer. Behind him, the landscape of the Somerset Levels stretches out, illuminated by the sunshine that peeps through the clouds.

The figure looks strong, and uncompromising. He is like a guardian of the gateway which leads into a new beginning. The staffs above his head appear to halt you, to stop you in your tracks before you can approach too close to him. The message he brings you is that you are on the threshold of new experience, and are about to enter a new dimension in your life. Before this can happen, there is a need to pause while you look back at your life, at the events which have brought you to this point. Reflect on these, and assimilate them. We can only move forward comfortably if we are unhampered by past baggage. Once this is accomplished, the guardian will lower the staffs and allow you to pass through.

The Staffs are held in the shape of a rune, Gebo, which means a gift or a kiss. This signifies that the new world that is opening up to you has gifts and opportunities to offer you. It is now time to accept these, and move joyfully forward.

DIVINATORY MEANING

You are standing on the threshold of new experience. Before you move forward into this, it is important that you first look back and come to terms with the past, for it has brought you to this point. Give thanks for what you have learned, and move with confidence towards the new opportunities that are being offered.

3 OF STAFFS
HONESTY

THE IMAGE

A man walks up the slopes of Wearyall Hill. He holds a staff in each hand, and they seem to be glowing and providing support. Behind him, a third staff rests in the ground, acting as a marker. In the distance, the Tor casts shadows in the early evening sun. The sky is yellow, symbolising hope, and the ability to observe and discriminate using the faculties of the mind.

The man's face is open, and enquiring. He looks expectantly at you as if you are an old friend who is waiting to ask a question. His clothes are shades of blue, the colour of peace and tranquillity, and spiritual harmony.

DIVINATORY MEANING

The Three of Staffs symbolises honesty in your dealings with others. It shows that you can trust those around you, and feel centred, and rooted in the everyday experiences of your life. Your self-confidence is high, and you are uncompromising about what you believe in, because you know that it works for you. Goals can be accomplished because of your steadfastness and determination. This card signifies creative opportunities coming your way.

The Two of Staffs, Gateway, has opened the way to creative energy. This can now be utilised to fulfil the potential signified by the Three of Staffs.

4 OF STAFFS
HOMECOMING

THE IMAGE

A couple are illuminated by light that pours from an open archway surrounded by greenery. The man has just lifted the woman into his arms, and is about to turn and carry her over the threshold and into the light. Both are laughing, and there is an atmosphere of happiness, excitement, and celebration. This could be the beginning of their new life together, or a move into a new home.

The woman wears a blue dress, signifying that she has an inner sense of calm and centredness, despite the feeling of excitement that surrounds the image. The man's top is red, colour of the will, of positivity, and action. His trousers are a deep blue-purple, suggesting that he has the inner discipline needed to put plans into action.

Four staffs stand like guardians at the doorway into the light. They represent structure and form, and the need for strong foundations in order for future plans to be put into action.Tendrils of ivy grow upwards from them, and create a doorway into the archway of light.

The honesty and self-confidence of the 3 of Staffs has created the opening, and the possibility of positive change engendered by the 4 of Staffs.

DIVINATORY MEANING

The Four of Staffs represents a sense of completion; a stage of your life has drawn to a close, and now it is time to move forward into a fresh and exciting new beginning. You feel a sense of optimism, and a growing sense of freedom. Plans made can now be put into action. There is the potential for a new relationship, or deeper commitment in an existing relationship. A change of residence is also possible.

5 OF STAFFS
EMPOWERMENT

THE IMAGE

A cloaked man dances around a circle of five staffs. It is the deep of night; the sky behind him is dark, with spirals of energy swirling within it. His hands are raised skywards, channelling lightning down into himself, and into the centre of the circle of staffs. He is totally in tune with the elements, and therefore able to use their power. His skin shines blue from the lightning bolts, his hair flies in the wind, and his strong face is a mask of concentration.

The man's cloak is red, the colour of the life-energy that vitalises the body through the blood. It is also the colour of the will, and this figure is engaged in totally focussing his will in order to accomplish his goal. From within the cloak, flames are visible; he identifies himself with intense spiritual energy, and is aware that fire can harm and purify, and that it needs to be controlled in order for its energy to be harnessed constructively.

The figure dances close to a tree on Wearyall Hill. He knows that if the lightning moves out of his control it can strike the tree and cause immense damage. But his confidence in himself and his power will not entertain even a possibility that this could happen.

DIVINATORY MEANING

You are now becoming aware of your inner power, and are confident enough to know that you exercise control over important aspects of your life. This card denotes an attitude of fearlessness, and you can even enjoy battling out a situation, partly for the excitement of the adrenalin surge, and partly because you know that you will be the victor.

The Four of Staffs denotes a sense of completion, and of a new beginning. The Five of Staffs reveals that all you need to change your life, and make it what you want it to be, is confidence. The figure in the card is the figure of a Shaman - one who understands how to tap into his or her power, and who is able to surrender the body to the spirit temporarily in order to gain an overview. Through that clear vision, healing can be facilitated.

You are now on the brink of a transformation in your life. You may have felt that you have been battling with a hopeless situation. Relax, and have faith in yourself. Whatever you believe you can accomplish, you will be able to accomplish.

6 OF STAFFS
SUCCESS

THE IMAGE

A young man stands before five staffs topped by lush leaves. The two staffs on the right of the image symbolise the Gateway card, the experience of new opportunities. On the left, the three staffs represent Honesty, the sense of accomplishment and integrity. He holds above his head a single staff, representing the ace, which indicates new beginnings.

The previous card, Empowerment, showed the battle of the Self for power and accomplishment. In this image, it has come to an end. Success is guaranteed, and the figure raises his staff above his head in joy and celebration. Like the figure in the Five of Staffs, he wears the colour red, signifying life-energy and strong passions. He is surrounded by, and bathed in, golden-yellow light, indicating that the success he has attained is due to clear thinking and positivity.

DIVINATORY MEANING

This card denotes victory over obstacles, and a tremendous sense of achievement. There is cause for celebration, and a feeling of a huge influx of energy which will revitalise all aspects of your being. It denotes an end to struggle, and gives the feeling that the world is your oyster. It can mean passing exams, or being offered a new job. Certainly it indicates that your success in your endeavours is assured.

7 OF STAFFS
COURAGE

THE IMAGE

A man stands by a blazing fire, barefoot, with a determined expression on his face. His hair flies in the wind as he throws a staff into the fire, which is already consuming another six staffs that he has already cast within it. The light of determination shines from him. Around him, Chalice Hill is dark, lit only by a few stars. It is the time of the dark moon, when it is hidden from view - the time of cleansing and purifying.

The gifts and opportunities offered by The Six of Staffs are about to be taken up. Nothing can hold you back now except your attachment to the past emotional and mental baggage that we all carry within us. The figure transfers these attachments into the staffs, and throws them into the fire, visualising them being dissolved and transmuted into positive energy. When we let go of the past, we are freed of unhelpful habit patterns, and can more easily put everything in its correct perspective.

DIVINATORY MEANING

The Seven of Staffs clears the ground for us, and helps us to make more space in our lives for what we truly want to manifest. To admit past mistakes or pain can take courage, yet this is a necessary part of the growth process, and frees us up to fully immerse ourselves in life.

You are now being given a chance to face up to, and dissolve, issues that have caused you problems in the past. In order to accomplish this, it is important that you allow yourself some time alone to think about what needs to be resolved. Then you can draw on your inner power, and consciously let go. A fresh way of thinking and being is opening up to you.

8 OF STAFFS
DIRECTNESS

THE IMAGE

An archer stands poised to shoot an arrow. His face and stance denote great concentration and inner as well as outer balance. His top is a burnt orange colour, signifying positivity and confidence. His trousers are dark green, suggesting that his energy is firmly grounded in the earth.

The slopes of Wearyall Hill rise behind him. To his left stands a tree that he has been using for target practice. Each arrow shot has hit the centre of the target. His aim is true, and he knows now that he is able to accomplish his goal. The arrow he holds is now aimed at his true target - out of our vision, as we each have our own personal goals.

The Seven of Staffs gave us the courage to clear away all hindrances. In this card, this has now been achieved, and we are able to allow the arrow of our will to hit the mark of our desire.

DIVINATORY MEANING

The Eight of Staffs indicates that your approach needs to be direct. Changes are occurring within you and around you, and you need to be focused and clear about what you want.

This is a time of swift movement, and of news coming imminently that will bring you joy. Clear, direct communication is vital, as you are now ready to achieve your goals, and with correct use of the will, they will be realised. The arrows symbolised by this card can also be the arrows of love. Someone may be about to enter your life with whom you will feel a strong affinity.

9 OF STAFFS
STRENGTH

9 OF STAFFS
STRENGTH

THE IMAGE

A man stands guarding a line of trees screening an area of intense light. He holds a staff as if to block your way forward, and his face is stern and uncompromising. He wears green, merging with the colours of the wooded area in which he stands. The darker greens represent being grounded in the earth energy, while the lighter greens signify a state of inner balance, harmony, creativity and healing. The trees' branches intertwine, representing the interdependence of all living things.

DIVINATORY MEANING

The Nine of Staffs represents our inner strength, which knows what we are, and are not, capable of. It prevents us from over-reaching ourselves. The Eight of Staffs showed us that all we needed to attain our goal was clear focus. With the Nine, we feel a need to protect what we have gained.

You are now becoming aware of your inner strength, and your potential. With the achievements you have experienced so far, you may be feeling frightened of losing, or having taken from you, what you have gained. Relax. You are now more able to use your keen perception to recognise those who are envious of your success, and you know how to intuit whether or not you can trust someone enough to allow them to get close to you. You are now able to act as guardian to the boundaries you choose to create.

10 OF STAFFS
RESPONSIBILITY

10 OF STAFFS
RESPONSIBILITY

THE IMAGE

A man stands in a garden, laughing at the baby held up in his arms. The baby's body is relaxed, and she gazes back at him. The man wears a dark blue top, symbolising the planet Saturn, which teaches us how to accept responsibility and work through our limitations. His trousers are grey, the colour of neutrality. The baby's outfit is pink, the colour of unconditional love.

Around them stretches a lawn; no flowers can be seen, which indicates that the man's life is taken up with the bare essentials at the moment. The seeds are within the earth still, they will emerge and blossom when the time and the season is right, but for now, the new life in the man's arms takes up all his time and energy.

Behind the figures is a hedge, denoting the ability, and the necessity, to create boundaries in your life. A gate formed from ten staffs leads out into the countryside, to new horizons. To the left, a tree casts its shadow across to the figures, signifying the need to keep your energy grounded in practicalities.

DIVINATORY MEANING

The Ten of Staffs relates to accepting responsibility. This can be seen as negative or positive, depending on your perspective. The Nine of Staffs taught the courage that is gained from recognising your inner strength, and creating healthy boundaries. The Ten of Staffs takes this a step further. It shows the necessity to take full responsibility for what we bring into our lives, with the knowledge that we always have a choice in how we view it and deal with it.

In some tarot decks, The Ten of Staffs is depicted as a man carrying a heavy burden of rods in his arms. He is bowed down uncomfortably. Yet if he was to shift the weight and carry it on his back, it would be far easier to carry. In that image, he does not recognise that he has a choice.

In the image depicted in this card, the man holds the baby easily. He knows that babies can take a great deal of time and energy, but he also understands the great joy and rewards incurred through watching and participating in the growth of a new and unique life.

In a reading, this card encourages you to look at the responsibilities you have, and how you perceive them. If they seem to be a burden, look at how you can ease this and make it more comfortable for yourself. Try taking a new perspective. Responsibility helps us to grow. It shows us that we are adults now, who can experience and celebrate who and what we are. And it is a great teacher. We are always capable of more than we think we can cope with.

MAID OF STAFFS

THE IMAGE

The Maid of Staffs stands on the very edge of the summit of Glastonbury Tor. The ground is a long way below, but she is unafraid of falling. She is naked; she has no illusions, and no barrier between herself and the rest of the world. In her supreme confidence, she is liberated from all bonds, and stands like an Amazon, a warrior woman, holding her staff as if to shake her defiance at the sky.

In her left hand, the hand of intuition, she holds a silk scarf that swirls like flame, reflected in her flowing hair. This is the flame of inspiration, of creative energy, and of passion. She is wild and untameable, truly in her power. All her fears have been overcome; nothing can stop her from achieving whatever she sets out to accomplish. She is an image of the raw, ungovernable force within ourselves which shouts a huge Yes! to life.

DIVINATORY MEANING

The Maid of Staffs signals that you now feel free enough, and confident enough, to be truly yourself. You have experienced the responsibilities of The Ten of Staffs, have vanquished your fears, and now know that nothing is impossible. There is a feeling of childlike optimism for the future - you know that your needs will be met.

This card can also signify a message, or a messenger, coming your way, which brings good news, and renewed hope. It can mean a steadfast friend or lover whom you can trust because they recognise their own inner power, and feel respect for yours. You do not need support, because you are aware of your own inner strength, and you are in the process of attracting others to you who are equally strong and independent.

KNIGHT OF STAFFS

KNIGHT OF STAFFS

THE IMAGE

The Knight of Staffs walks with his eyes focused straight ahead. His face is lit by the clouds which reflect the glowing colours of the rising sun. He looks intent, yet there is a dreamy quality to be seen in his eyes.

In his hand he carries a staff that bears many leaves, symbol of a blossoming process taking place. His tunic is a warm peach colour, the colour of gentle love, and it is gored through with extra fabric in red, which signifies the will, action and passion, and yellow, symbolising understanding.

DIVINATORY MEANING

The fearlessness of The Maid of Staffs has allowed her to be open to the new and untried. The Knight brings fresh energy, new and intense emotional experiences, and an exciting blossoming of creativity and intuition. He signifies that events are moving swiftly forward in a positive manner, and your experience of this card will be an increasing sense of eagerness.

There is an urge to explore your possibilities, to move onwards, to travel within your inner space, or express this outwardly by making changes in your life.

QUEEN OF STAFFS

QUEEN OF STAFFS

THE IMAGE

The Queen of Staffs stands poised at the top of Ebbor Gorge. She has travelled a long and arduous path to reach her goal, but now it is attained, she is able to rest at the summit, and shade her eyes with her hand while she decides in which direction she wishes to move.

The landscape behind her is beautiful, but wild and mountainous. To climb the steep and rocky slopes takes stamina and courage, but the incredible views from the top are well worth the effort.

The Queen's hair is a bright auburn shade. It signifies strong emotions, powerfully expressed. Her cloak is a rich golden yellow, the colour of the sun, symbolising positivity, strength, courage, and a spiritual attitude towards life. She has experienced the intensity and passion of the Knight, and has undergone a transformation within herself that enables her to feel compassion for others. This is an image of someone who has welcomed life with open arms, embraced all experiences wholeheartedly, and learned from both the good and the difficult aspects, rejecting nothing.

DIVINATORY MEANING

You have experienced much in your life, and felt your emotions keenly. Because of your ability to be introspective, you have learned from your experiences, and have integrated this into your quest for self-knowledge. You are compassionate and kind, yet very strong in your views.

The Queen of Staffs also indicates mature sexual energy - not the infatuation of youth, but a need to be accepted as an equal in a relationship.

The long, hard way is now behind you. It is time to recharge yourself and assimilate what you have experienced and learned.

KING OF STAFFS

KING OF STAFFS

THE IMAGE

The King of Staffs moves swiftly against the wind, his cloak and hair blowing behind him. He is rejoicing in the elements, pushing against the wind that attempts, and fails, to hold him back.

The sky behind him is bright yellow, and glows on his face, which radiates happiness and delight. There is a feeling of great exhilaration, of moving forward and overcoming all odds. He is totally in tune with himself and his power.

The King's cloak is a vivid orange, symbolising positive energy, and deep inner joy. Clasping the neck of his cloak is a golden snake brooch, indicating that he is in harmony with both the sexual and spiritual aspects of himself, and can use each to fuel the energy of the other.

Whereas The Queen of Staffs reveals the compassion and self-knowledge that comes from direct experience, and the need to pause after a long journey, The King of Staffs is refreshed, and eager to begin anew. His dynamic personality will not allow for rest - change and new experience is what he seeks.

DIVINATORY MEANING

The King of Staffs indicates a time of great forward movement. There is an influx of energy that cannot be ignored; you are gripped by a feeling of excitement and impatience to make things happen, and life is responding to that urge by creating changes around you. You can now tap into the rising tide of eagerness and enthusiasm, overcome any difficult situations that may arise, and enable your leadership qualities to come to the fore.

This card shows strong-mindedness, and an indomitable will. There is an open honesty in your optimism that will attract other people to you, and enable your inspired ideas to be put into action.

ACE OF CHALICES
THE BLUE BOWL

ACE OF CHALICES
THE BLUE BOWL

The Blue Bowl is an artefact still shrouded in mystery. Its age is indeterminable, and its craftsmanship is very unusual, and difficult to date, so its age is still not known. The only certainty is that it is very old, and is made of blue glass, with a silver leaf pattern in amber and floral designs embedded within it.

It was discovered in Bordighera, Italy, by an English doctor, John Goodchild, who worked in Italy each winter. The Bowl was accompanied by a platter, but Goodchild had a strong feeling that the Bowl had a special, and mystical, significance. He brought it back to England, and received psychic instructions to place it in the muddy waters of Bride's Well, Glastonbury. This he did, and was informed through his visions that it would be found by a pure woman who would become its keeper.

Some years later, around 1906, he was visited by two sisters from Bristol, Janet and Christine Allen. They had found the Bowl at Bride's Well after being psychically directed there, washed it, and replaced it in the Well. Goodchild kept silent, and waited until Christine had a vision of a hand rising out of the water and offering her the Bowl to drink from. He took this as a sign that these were the true guardians, and told the story of the Bowl and his visions.

Janet returned alone to Bride's Well, and retrieved the Bowl. They created a sanctuary for it at their house in Bristol, and the Bowl was viewed by many of the leading psychics of that time who declared it to be the Grail. The scientific community were thrown into confusion because the Bowl defied analysis. It was discovered to have a healing effect on those who came to it, and was taken around the world with the idea of unifying East and West.

Eventually the Bowl was returned to Glastonbury, where it still resides under the guardianship of the trustees of Chalice Well.

THE IMAGE

The Blue Bowl floats in the centre of the card, light reflecting from within it. Around the Bowl is golden light, symbol of spiritual energy, spilling downwards like a fountain, and rising upwards to spread its energy all around. Coloured light emerges from the gold, in bands of green, blue and pink. The green signifies healing, sensitivity, and harmony. Blue represents devotion on a deep spiritual level, and pink symbolises the power and beauty of unconditional love.

Whatever the true origins of the Blue Bowl, it appears to have a potent power to inspire. It shines in the centre of the image, suggesting the harmony that is revealed through the union of its creator with the wellhead of inspiration that all artists aspire to.

DIVINATORY MEANING

The Ace of Chalices represents pure love, which overflows into every aspect of our existence. It suggests the ability to truly give and receive, with no thought of any possibility that the energy could dwindle, because there is the awareness that love is infinite and eternal, and can only grow through the experience of it. Love cannot be portioned out, it is freely available to all, and it is what we need, seek, and deserve as our birthright.

This card signifies the ability to tap into this great wellspring of life, to feel its power deep within ourselves, and to express it as best we can to those around us. In a reading, The Ace of Chalices shows you that love is freely available to you at this moment. A tide of bliss awaits you, a feeling of total connection with those around you. All you need to do is go with the flow, accept it, and give thanks for it.

2 OF CHALICES
LOVE

THE IMAGE

A couple stand gazing lovingly at each other, surrounded by the pink light of unconditional love, and gold light which signifies that their union is on the spiritual as well as physical level. Their colouring is in reverse to Creiddylad and Gwythyr in card 6, The Lovers. The woman has dark hair, and the man is fair. He wears green leggings, signifying balance, harmony and creativity; her dress is in shades of pink, denoting the unconditional and nurturing aspects of her love.

In their hands, they each clasp a golden chalice. Their arms and wrists are entwined, enabling each to drink from the cup of the other, to seal their pledge. Between the couple, rising from the chalices, is a shimmering umbilical cord which leads upward to a foetus in its sac surrounded by the petals of a pink flower. This signifies that when two people enter into a relationship, their combined energies create a third energy - that of the relationship itself - which, in healthy relationships, enables each individual to express the highest and most creative aspects of themselves. This does not necessarily indicate the birth of a physical child; it means the birth of new life, inspiration, and understanding.

DIVINATORY MEANING

The Two of Chalices indicates the beginning of a new and beautiful relationship, which will bring you great joy. The sense of overflowing love for the universe symbolised by the Ace of Chalices has now found a focus, and is channelled into another human being. Within existing relationships, this card signifies an increase in the flow of love between you, and a cementing of your union, either as a live-in relationship, or as marriage.

This is a time when new and exciting links with other people are being forged; there is increased harmony in friendships. This card reminds you that if you allow yourself to love yourself, others will find it easy to love you.

3 OF CHALICES
CELEBRATION

3 OF CHALICES
CELEBRATION

THE IMAGE

Three young children dressed as a fairy and two pixies dance in a circle on the slopes of Chalice Hill. Their hands are held high in the air, and they smile widely at each other, revelling in the moment. The grass below their feet is illuminated by their presence, like a magic circle, and flowers spring from it. Three chalices stand in a wide triangular shape, opening out towards them, allowing yet more energy to enter the sacred space they have created.

The girl wears pink, symbolic of love in its most unconditional form. She wears a circlet of flowers on her head, and more flowers are entwined in her hair. Flowers exude their fragrance and beauty whether or not anyone notices them; they are content to be purely what they are.

The younger boy wears yellow shorts and an orange top, signifying an abundance of energy and happiness. The older boy wears shades of blue - he is learning the elements of self control, and has temporarily dropped his feelings of wanting to be grown up, in order to join in the fun. The image signifies the childlike element within ourself which still needs to play, no matter what age we are.

The Two of Chalices hinted at the energy created from a relationship. The Three of Chalices shows the expression of joy that is gained through exploration of that energy.

DIVINATORY MEANING

The Three of Chalices indicates an abundance of love between a small group of people. It brings energy to close friendships, and to families. There is cause for celebration - new opportunities are coming your way that you can rejoice in, and which will enable you to share your good fortune with others. An abundance of rich life experiences is on its way, and there is a sense of great happiness.

This card encourages you to be more in touch with your inner child - the part of you that needs to laugh, play, have fun, and be sociable. Perhaps you have been taking life too seriously. It is now time to lighten up and enjoy it!

4 OF CHALICES
EMOTION

THE IMAGE

A young woman stands framed in the arbour of a garden on Wearyall Hill. It is early evening, the light is beginning to fade around her, casting the trees into dark shadows. A radiance emanates from within her form, and illuminates the roses that bloom on the archway around her. She holds the supports for the plants, and flowers seem to be falling towards her feet. At the base of the image, four chalices rest in the grass.

The woman wears a wreath of leaves in her hair, symbolising her attunement with the cycles of nature. Her tights are green, the colour of creative energy, intuition, and inner balance. Her purple skirt shows her awareness of the spiritual aspects of her nature, and the red top denotes an abundance of energy and vitality. A blue waistcoat is just visible - she is devoted to those she loves, and gives much in return.

DIVINATORY MEANING

The Four of Chalices shows the support of those around you, which enables you to feel nourished and cherished. You give a great deal of yourself to those whom you care for, and are able to receive love in return. As with The Three of Chalices, there is a childlike quality within this card, a sense of innocence.

It is important that you enjoy the support of others, without allowing yourself to rely on it. It is good to have, but there is a need for you to be able to stand alone and know that your strength truly comes from within yourself, and not from those around you. By realising this, you are able to resist any temptation to lean on others, or to allow them to lean too heavily on you, and through this a healthy balance of energy can be maintained.

5 OF CHALICES
PROGRESSION

5 OF CHALICES
PROGRESSION

THE IMAGE

A woman walks up Chalice Hill towards two golden chalices that sit together on the higher slopes. Her cloak is a dark purple, associated with mourning, and it trails behind her. She holds it close to her upper body, hugging its warmth around her.

The wind blows her hair, and sends clouds scurrying across the sky. It is winter, the trees are bare and the scene has a bleakness to it. Dark storm clouds at the lower left of the image are being blown away, to be replaced by lighter clouds, and then patches of blue sky over the top of the hill and the chalices she is moving towards.

DIVINATORY MEANING

Behind her are three silver chalices, all overturned. They represent the lunar energy, the emotions, which have been spilt. The woman has experienced great disappointment, she feels fragile and heavy inside. But the gold chalices before her are solar energies; they represent hope and wholeness. The two standing together signify duality; once the woman reaches them, she will have the inner clarity to see both sides of the situation she has left behind, and will be able to acknowledge what she has gained as well as what she has lost. These two chalices also offer a hint of her future - the next card in the tarot sequence is The Six of Chalices, Union.

The Four of Chalices indicates a need to not lean too much on the emotional support of others. If not learned, this lesson is revealed through the image on The Five of Chalices. Disappointment has been experienced, and the urge now is to seek wholeness and healing from within the self.

6 OF CHALICES
UNION

6 OF CHALICES
Union

THE IMAGE

Two lovers kiss on the slopes of Chalice Hill. It is early evening, and the setting sun paints the Tor purple and the sky in radiant pinks, reds and yellows. The passion depicted in the image is felt on all levels of being. The lovers are experiencing a sensual, emotional and spiritual union that will sustain them for long after this moment.

The man leans towards the woman, and she reaches up to him, smiling as he kisses her. There is a similarity in their appearance, they are like mirror-images of each other, and each of them sees the beauty in each other.

The woman's dress reflects the sunset colours on the Tor. The six buttons on its front are in the shape of chalices. She is in tune with herself, and in harmony with nature, and feels a sense of perfection and anticipation in this moment. The man wears a blue vest, denoting his deep love and devotion.

DIVINATORY MEANING

The Six of Chalices signifies great pleasure to be gained from a relationship. The disappointment of The Five of Chalices has been overcome, and it is now time to allow yourself to freely give and receive. Love is being expressed on all levels, and can now be fully explored.

There is an attitude of trust, and an increasing sense of discovery as you move into the urge to unite and merge with another. This brings to light aspects of yourself that previously remained hidden from view, and you are able to delight in the deeper knowledge that you are experiencing of yourself and your partner.

This card indicates a sudden and powerful attraction between yourself and another, that will enrich all areas of your life. It signifies experiences of tantra - of being able to channel sexual energy in such a way that it also empowers you spiritually.

7 OF CHALICES
FANTASY

7 OF CHALICES
FANTASY

THE IMAGE

The symbolism of Union depicted in The Six of Chalices now leads into a connection with the inner nature. A woman in an iridescent robe reaches out to touch one of seven chalices which float in the sky above her. Each chalice is a colour of the rainbow, and they also correspond to the seven chakras, or energy centres, of the body. Their colours denote aspects of being which can be expressed through the personality. The blue chalice which radiates light into the woman is the colour of communication - she and the chalice are each in communion with the other; she is able to contact her intuition and her inner vision, and use the insights gained through this.

The garden in which she stands is a surreal vision of Chalice Well Garden. The bushes, trees and flowers all glow with an otherworldly radiance, and there is an unearthly, ethereal quality to the image. All is vividly beautiful, because we have the power to create this in our lives through focusing on our dreams and bringing them into existence. The woman's robe shimmers with the reflected light of the colours around her, indicating that we are able to express all aspects of ourselves outwardly if only we can believe in our ability to do so.

DIVINATORY MEANING

This card shows that you have the ability to tap into your fantasy life, and choose what you wish to focus on and manifest in your everyday life. There is a need to be able to discriminate between what is a dream, that can be used for inspiration, and what is an illusion, with no possibility of being grounded in reality.

Dreams are very necessary to our existence. They help us to bring the unlikely into the realms of the possible. You have the knowledge that a dream can become reality, you understand the gifts of dreaming, and you can now use that ability to enable yourself to realise a vision that inspires you.

8 OF CHALICES
RENEWAL

8 OF CHALICES
RENEWAL

THE IMAGE

On Chalice Hill, a young girl begins to remove her cloak. It is dark blue on the outside, and has contained and protected her energy while she was feeling vulnerable. But the lining that is becoming visible is radiant with hues of blue, violet, and pink - all aspects of her personality that she has hidden from the view of others until now. The blues indicate her wish to communicate her needs; the violet is her blossoming connection to the deep, inner aspects of herself; and the pink is her growing self-love and acceptance, which enables her to feel and express this to others around her.

The clothes revealed beneath the cloak are multi-coloured, and in many layers. She is becoming aware of the vast potential of who she truly is, instead of how she thinks others see her. All the facets of her personality are now becoming known to her, and she can now choose which of those she wants to employ, and who she wishes to be. The mask that she held over her face is now lowered; she no longer needs to hide from the world, though she can choose to retreat from it if she wishes.

Behind the figure stand eight chalices, looking very small against the backdrop of Chalice Hill. She is moving away from past fears, and from others' expectations of her, and turns towards the glowing path of light that is illuminated by the sun's rays. The path will lead her towards the sun that shines above the hill, and therefore towards a new confidence and an increase of positive energy.

DIVINATORY MEANING

The Eight of Chalices indicates that it is time to say farewell to old, outworn patterns of behaviour. The ability to allow yourself to dream that is signified by The Seven of Chalices has enabled you to free yourself up, to become aware that there are many different aspects to you, and that it can be fun, as well as liberating, to explore them.

There is a sense of discovery, and of playfulness. You are now aware that you can choose the mask, or persona, that you present to the world, but that this is only a small part of who you really are. You are now free to experiment with the many diverse aspects of yourself, to become an explorer of your inner self, and to revel in the freedom that you feel.

9 OF CHALICES
GENEROSITY

THE IMAGE

A beautiful child holds a chalice as if offering it to you. She smiles shyly, and her face is illuminated by the light that shines upwards from the chalice. The light radiates around her head, and spills over her shoulders and down to the ground like a fountain, and within its depths are eight smaller chalices.

The child's hair is white, a symbol of purity and innocence. Her dress is the green of compassion, of healing and balance - and of love and abundance. Behind her is the golden glow from the chalice which reflects her own giving nature, radiating outwards to the vivid orange of positive energy, happiness, and fulfilment. The freedom to explore all aspects of yourself denoted by The Eight of Chalices has now shifted into a state of total composure and the knowledge that you have within you an infinite range of possibilities. This leads to the realisation that the more you give, the more you receive, and the universe is benevolent and abundant.

DIVINATORY MEANING

This card signifies open-heartedness. Your ability to accept others as they are, without judgement, and with no expectations of them, gives you an endearing quality that draws people to you. Because you are able to function from your heart energy, the universe responds by enabling you to accept its gifts while you offer your own gifts of love and compassion to others.

This is a time of abundance, a time when your dreams are about to be realised, filling you with a sense of blessedness. Allow yourself to enjoy what is offered to you, without questioning it, because it is your own positive energy that is finding its way back to you. A healing is taking place on many levels, so let yourself celebrate the bounty of life.

10 OF CHALICES
HAPPINESS

10 OF CHALICES
HAPPINESS

THE IMAGE

A woman stands in the iron-rich waters of Chalice Well. Her hands are raised in delight and wonder as the waterfall cascades down to swirl and eddy around her legs. Light shines out from the source of the water's flow in the same way as the source of our being is radiant light. The slabs of stone that channel the water glow with subtle tones from its rich iron content, one of the necessities of life.

Three chalices, representing the card Celebration, stand at the base of the first waterfall, resting on the ledge above the source of light. The other seven chalices, shown in the card Fantasy, form an X shape around the woman, the universal symbol for a kiss.

The face of the woman radiates delight and openness. Her soft green clothing represents inner harmony and balance, and expresses her fundamentally creative nature. Her hair flows freely down her back; she feels supported by the universe, and in tune with all her desires and needs, knowing that these will be met because of her trusting nature.

The Generosity of The Nine of Chalices is now fulfilling its promise, and the woman in this image is now able to express her deepest feelings and allow herself to be receptive to the gifts of love.

DIVINATORY MEANING

The Ten of Chalices indicates a time of great happiness. All your efforts have been rewarded, and the world is viewed as a place of great beauty. You are now open to love, and feel a sense of connection to the universe and to the people around you. You are able to tap into the wellspring of happiness and deep joy that comes from the very essence of your inner being.

A feeling of great fulfilment is present, and your imagination can now grow wings and fly you to new and undreamed-of heights of bliss. You are in touch with an area of inner mystery within yourself. This is a time of heightened creativity in every area of your life.

MAID OF CHALICES

MAID OF CHALICES

THE IMAGE

A young woman sits cross-legged on Bride's Mound surrounded by poppies, a symbol of surrender, joy, and heightened states of awareness. She holds a chalice at heart level as if inviting you to drink from it. Her dress is blue, the colour of devotion and centredness. The sleeves hang loosely down to her lap - she is able to be flexible, and is open-hearted. The front of her dress is loosely laced; she knows how to contain her emotional energy, yet still is willing to give freely of herself.

DIVINATORY MEANING

The Maid of Chalices represents the ability to give freely of yourself. There is a kind of innocence in this card; life holds a feeling of freshness and purity. You are receptive to the energies and feelings of others, and can rely on your intuition to know whom you can or cannot trust. Your sensitivity is heightened. This is a time of hope, when the fulfilment of The Ten of Chalices can be enjoyed without being taken for granted.

KNIGHT OF CHALICES

THE IMAGE

From the waters of the Somerset Levels, a young man wades towards you. His face wears an expression of intensity, and his eyes have the ability to look deep into your soul. His tunic is white, the colour of purity and innocence, and also of blossoming potential. He gently holds a shining golden chalice, engraved with a rising snake. Out of the bowl of the chalice itself emerges a real snake, coloured red and green, the colours of desire and love. The snake seems to be moving towards the area of his heart, signifying an awakening of the emotions. The young man does not seem to notice the snake; his focus is directly on you as he moves towards you.

The water reaches the level of the base chakra, the seat of the desires. The young man is beginning to understand his feelings, but is still driven by them. Whereas The Maid of Chalices indicates heightened sensitivity to the emotional life, and to others, The Knight needs to explore all of the possibilities that union with another can bring.

DIVINATORY MEANING

You are now learning to recognise, and act on, your desires. This card can indicate the beginning of a romantic encounter, where as yet there is no desire for commitment. An exploration of all the possibilities is present, along with a growing sense of how you can recognise and integrate your deepest emotions.

The Knight of Chalices brings the realisation that both the wisdom and the sexuality aspects of a relationship need to be explored, symbolised in the image by the snake. Desire can burn out quickly unless it is backed up by a connection based on a common goal and the ability to communicate. This card denotes a deeper exploration of the Self, and the need to communicate your desires and wishes clearly, in order to see them fulfilled.

QUEEN OF CHALICES

THE IMAGE

At the top of Ebbor Gorge, a woman holds a chalice engraved with a heart. She smiles broadly, and offers the chalice as if it is a part of herself. Her dress is the pink shade of unconditional love, and flows over her voluptuous body to settle on the ground around her, signifying that she is centred in her emotions and offers them freely to all who come to her.

Behind her, trees in full leaf show that she is firmly rooted within herself, and is able to express her inner nature openly and honestly. The distant fields and hills are verdant shades of green, displaying their bounty and preparing to nourish those who tend them.

The Knight of Chalices represented the blossoming of desire, without the need for instant commitment. The Queen has taken this further, to indicate an ability to be totally committed to those she loves. She gives freely of herself, and represents an ideal of womanhood and motherhood, much like The Empress card. But where The Empress is still ruled by her passions, The Queen of Chalices integrates them into herself and aims to differentiate between passion and love.

DIVINATORY MEANING

The Queen of Chalices signifies that you are now ready and willing to give fully of yourself in an unconditional way. You have the ability to relate to your deepest feelings, and to express them through your creative and imaginative faculties. There is the need to both give and receive love, as it is a cornerstone of your existence. You know what you want, and how to go about getting it.

KING OF CHALICES

THE IMAGE

The sun rises over the Somerset Levels, casting coloured reflections from the trees and sky onto the still water. A noble Palamino horse carries its rider along the shore. The man sits on his horse in a relaxed manner, his curly hair flowing behind him. He carries a chalice in his left hand, the hand of intuition, while his unseen right hand holds the reins. He is able to guide the horse using his reason, and at the same time is deeply in tune with his intuitive, feeling nature.

The horse's reins are a deep cerise pink, and so is the cloth across its back - the colour of the highest expression of the emotions. The King wears green leggings, symbolising his attunement with his heart-energy and creativity. His tunic is the blue of devotion, with a pale blue belt. His face wears a wide grin - he could be laughing, or singing; and certainly he is allowing his happiness to bubble up from its depths and be expressed. There is an air about him of a man on his way to a tryst with his lover.

The King of Chalices is a perfect match for his counterpart, The Queen. Both are full-blooded and open, and both have a deep-seated need to express their emotions, and to seek an equal partnership with their ideal mate.

DIVINATORY MEANING

The King of Chalices represents the image of the ideal man - someone who is passionate about life, who freely expresses his emotions, and who is able to be touched by them on all levels of being - physical, emotional, mental and spiritual. For a woman, this card can mean an ideal love entering her life, or being present in it already. For a man, it shows ability, and desire, to enter wholeheart-edly into a relationship, with a sense of joy and commitment.

This card also represents an offer being made to you by a man who is in tune with his creativity. It can denote a patron of the arts. It suggests that you can trust any guidance, or offers made to you, as these are likely to bring you success in your undertakings.

THE ACE OF SWORDS
EXCALIBUR

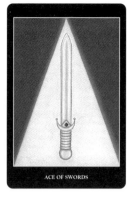

ACE OF SWORDS

Excalibur, the famous sword of King Arthur, was forged at the request of Merlin and the Ladies of the Lake by the Faery-Folk of Avalon. Its blade was said to bring instant death. Its scabbard had the power to staunch the flow of blood, and heal wounds. It was received by Arthur from a mysterious hand that rose above the waters of the Lake, and the sword was his constant companion. His death came about because the scabbard had been stolen from him. At the death of Arthur, Bedivere threw Excalibur into the Lake from whence it had come, and watched as a hand rose from the water, grasped the sword by its hilt, and drew it back under the surface.

THE IMAGE

Excalibur rises, bathed in a triangle of golden light, surrounded by intense blue. The yellow-gold signifies the power of thought, and sharp intellect married with a deep connection to the spirit. Blue is the colour of devotion to a high ideal, and also represents clarity and the ability to create space around you - both on the inner and outer levels.

The blade of the sword shines silver, while the hilt is gold, symbolising the unification of the sun and the moon - the intuition and the intellect. To use a sword effectively, there is a need to be attuned psychically, to be able to 'feel out' where your opponent is likely to strike. You also need to use the solar aspects of logic and right use of the will in order to act effectively. The sun and the moon are also represented by the solar disc on the handle of the sword, and the curved lunar shape on its hilt, topped by a tiny representation of the sun and the full moon - symbolising the total integration of the conscious and unconscious mind.

The seven rings on the hilt represent the seven planes of matter common to all philosophies. An amethyst set at the base of the blade signifies clear, concise thought, and compassion. It is also a stone of protection.

DIVINATORY MEANING

The Ace of Swords signifies the need, and the ability, for clear, concise thinking. It is related to knowledge, and the power of reasoning. You are now able to act decisively, and to easily cut through obstacles in order to reach your goal. This card indicates great success because you have been able to thoroughly think things through.

You are able to express yourself clearly, so that others will listen to your ideas and take them seriously. Your powers of reasoning are infallible, as they are supported by your ability to sense any undercurrents that are going on in those around you.

2 OF SWORDS
EQUILIBRIUM

2 OF SWORDS
EQUILIBRIUM

THE IMAGE

Against a backdrop of stars, a man stands with his arms crossed and two short swords held in his hands. His eyes are closed, and his face looks peaceful, even meditative. Light shines from him, creating a vivid glow against the night sky.

His tunic is the soft green shade that denotes the heart energy, the intuition, and the creative aspects of the self - all blending to create a delicate balance and harmony. His arms are crossed over his heart, protecting the emergence of tender feelings, and a pink glow, signifying love, radiates gently from that area. He is protecting that energy in order to nurture it until it is strong enough to be expressed without any danger of being destroyed.

The swords he holds are almost small enough to be daggers. He presents no threat to those around him, yet is able to fend off with a sharp thrust, those who come too close to his sacred space and disturb his new-found tranquillity.

The equilibrium he has found is still fragile and delicate. It needs to be fostered by time alone with himself, so that he can discover how to be able to integrate it fully within himself, and carry it within him in the outside world.

DIVINATORY MEANING

The Two of Swords indicates a need to contact a state of balance and inner peace within yourself in order to work in harmony with your own needs and desires. You feel the need to protect your heart energy while a healing process takes place within you.

This is a time to look within yourself for answers, to listen to what your heart is telling you that you need. The Ace of Swords signifies action based on the intellect, and victory over obstacles. The Two of Swords shows that action always needs to be balanced by a period of rest and introspection so that more energy can then be gathered in, and deeper self-knowledge can be attained.

3 OF SWORDS
GRIEF

THE IMAGE

On Chalice Hill, three figures are poised, all facing away from each other. The colours in this card are dark, and the night sky is black and devoid of stars. In the centre of the image is a yellow inverted triangle. It symbolises great mental energy being used wrongly - the pure and clear focus of the triangle is being distorted. Instead of pointing upwards towards clarity, it points down, so that its energy is not available for positive use.

At each point of the triangle is a figure cloaked in the dark red of desire. Two of the figures are standing, turning away from each other, linked at the base chakra, the centre of sexual desire and the survival mechanism. The third figure at the apex of the triangle is seated on the ground, linked to the other two people in the area of the head - the thoughts. Their faces are hidden by their hoods; they cannot show their thoughts or intentions. Each figure holds a sword, leaning dejectedly upon it as it rests in a pool of water created by their tears. The tips of the swords are immersed in the water, making their sharp edges which can cut through obstacles, useless.

The state of Equilibrium shown in The Two of Swords has not been maintained, and the three figures are thrown off balance, and are unable to find a solution. Yet if you look clearly at the image, the solution can be seen there. The figures are not in communication with each other; they are driven by their needs and desires, to the exclusion of rationality. All three are linked - this could be an unhappy triangular relationship, or a situation of having to make a difficult choice between two people in your life.

What is now needed is for the three people to turn and face each other honestly and directly. By looking into the illuminated triangle, and communicating, the energy can be turned around and a solution found. The swords can be lifted above the water in order that their qualities of insight and their ability to cut through situations can be employed. This is not easy, but it is necessary.

DIVINATORY MEANING

The Three of Swords indicates a difficult situation that is fuelled by jealousy, or the feeling that someone is trying to take what you see as belonging to you. There is a sense of dejection and loss, and you are unable to see a clear way through.

There is a need to stop looking inward, and to dissolve any feelings of blame. The way forward is to try to understand what is actually going on, though this may be painful. A degree of severance is required, and a need to accept the outcome of the situation, with the awareness that what is truly yours will eventually come back to you, if you allow yourself to let go of expectations.

4 OF SWORDS
RECUPERATION

4 OF SWORDS
RECUPERATION

THE IMAGE

The sun rises over the top of Wearyall Hill, and casts its light over a sleeping figure who lies on the grass. Four swords rest in a square shape around him, protecting him from anything or anyone who would disturb his slumber.

The man sprawls on the grass, his head resting against his hands as if he would guard his dream-space. He wears only grey-blue trousers, which have ridden up to expose his lower legs, and his feet, which symbolise the soul's connection to the earth, are bare. The scene is peaceful and tranquil after the image of pain depicted in The Three of Swords. The crisis is over, and he can now rest and replenish himself.

DIVINATORY MEANING

The Four of Swords indicates a time of rest and respite, a period of retreat from the demands of the world, in order to integrate events that have been taking place in your life. You need some time to build up your energy, as a lot of effort has been expended up to this point, and rest, or a brief break from routine, is needed in order for you to recharge your batteries.

You could choose to spend some time alone, or go away for a holiday or even a weekend, so that you can be in a position where no demands are made on you. You have given a great deal of yourself, and now the time has come to focus on your own needs.

5 OF SWORDS
ACCEPTANCE

THE IMAGE

The setting sun paints the sky in luminous tones of gold, scarlet, blues and purples, and reflects its light over the Mendip Hills. In the foreground a woman is seated, her posture serene, her feet bare. Her golden hair shines in the evening light, and reflects the inner light that comes from the stillness of her being.

The woman's face is calm and still, as if she is meditating. Yet there is also a sadness in her expression, and in the way her hands hold a piece of scarlet cloth - the colour of life-energy, of passion, and of anger. Her bearing is upright, aided by the rigidity of the bodice of her blouse. She needs this in order to remain upright, to keep her spine, that which supports her, in a position of strength. The sleeves of her blouse, in contrast, are loose and flowing - gathered at the shoulders, the area of responsibility, and falling to her wrists.

Her blouse is purple, the colour of spiritual awareness, and also the colour of grief. Her blue skirt signifies devotion, and inner peace.

Behind the woman is a piece of scarlet cloth, pierced by five swords. It looks almost like spilled blood, and signifies emotional pain connected with loss. Another, identical piece of cloth is held in her hands, symbolising that with any situation, there is always something to gain, or to learn. She is allowing herself to sit with her feelings, to acknowledge them and absorb them in order to be able to release any pain or disappointment. With acceptance comes a sense of peace and tranquillity that will enable her to open herself to new possibilities.

DIVINATORY MEANING

The Five of Swords indicates the ending of a struggle that has been taking place in your life. The period of rest indicated by The Four of Swords has paved the way to fresh insights, and an acceptance of what you have.

By letting go of the past, and allowing yourself to move in a new direction, a sense of empowerment manifests itself. You are now ready to make positive changes in your life. This is a time when you need to centre yourself, and nurture yourself, in order to recover from inner wounds or a past situation of abuse.

The sun has now set on the old. It is time to rest, and watch the sunrise that heralds the dawn of new experience. Your own inner light shines through you, and provides you with the protection you need.

6 OF SWORDS
PERCEPTION

6 OF SWORDS
PERCEPTION

THE IMAGE

A man looks piercingly at you as he holds his hands above his head, forming a triangular shape with his thumbs and forefingers. The triangle represents clarity and perception, and his head is bathed in its light, indicating that his mental processes are honed to perfection. The light created by the triangle spills downwards, lightening the colour of his denim shirt, to form a diamond shape. The man is inviting us to look at the world in a new way, to explore hitherto undreamed-of possibilities.

Six swords decorate his shirt, all pointing upwards in order to increase the flow of energy. Their hilts are a luminous green, signalling us to listen to our intuition. The swords are aimed in pairs, one pair pointing at the solar plexus area, the part of our body where the will emerges from; the second pair aims towards the heart, the area of feeling; and the third pair points towards the throat, the area of communication.

The Acceptance of The Five of Swords has now led into a new, focused way of seeing and thinking. Insights come flowing freely into our minds, accompanied by the energy to put those insights into action.

DIVINATORY MEANING

You are striving to express realisations and truths that come from deep within yourself. You are now able to express your thoughts and ideas clearly and concisely, in a way that others can understand.

The old way of life is now being left behind; new horizons beckon you, and there is a sense of freshness and newness that is born from your need to investigate other, more liberating possibilities.

7 OF SWORDS
BOUNDARIES

7 OF SWORDS
BOUNDARIES

THE IMAGE

A couple sit on the grass at the base of Wearyall Hill, surrounded by seven swords. The swords are situated so that one stands immediately behind each figure, as if to give support; one stands in the centre, just behind their joined hands; and four others lie on the ground before them as if to create a boundary that others may not pass.

The man and woman both sit cross-legged, mirroring each other's body language. They are smiling, and seem comfortable with each other. Their clothes are also mirror-images. Both wear blue, the colour of devotion and clarity.

The swords are topped by a golden globe, representing the sun's energy. This brings growth and a sense of purpose to the relationship.

In any relationships with others, it is important to maintain a sense of individuality, and for both people involved to have a clear sense of boundaries in order for respect to be present. Indistinct or blurred boundaries create problems in that one of the people, at least, can feel put-upon or infringed on.

The boundaries made clearer by the Perception of The Six of Swords, should be viewed as a healthy aspect of any relationship. We can be close to others, but there is always a need to also be able to function self-reliantly.

DIVINATORY MEANING

This card reveals the ability to set boundaries for what you want and do not want in your life, yet still be able to be close to, and relate to other people. You are likely to feel stifled if your boundaries are overstepped. There is a need for you to retain your individuality, and claim your own sacred space. There is also the indication of respect for the sacred space of others.

Problems in relationships can now be resolved through clear direct communication, and through being centred within yourself, kindly but firmly stating your needs and how they could best be met. It is also important to listen to and respect the views of others who are in dialogue with you.

8 OF SWORDS
RELEASE

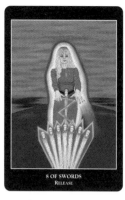

8 OF SWORDS
RELEASE

THE IMAGE

On Chalice Hill, against a blood-red sky flecked with black clouds, a woman stands erect, pouring energy through her hands into seven swords that are fixed into the ground in front of her. An eighth sword hangs from her belt. Her face is angry and determined, her neck muscles are tense with the effort of channelling her overwhelming emotions safely.

The woman wears a scarlet dress, the colour of anger, and also of positive life-energy. A small flame glows in her heart, signifying that although she has felt mistreated, there is still the space within her for compassion.

Around her is an aura of white, blue and violet light with yellow zig-zags emanating like lightning through it. This shows the power of thought-forms, and the empowerment that comes from being able to express every aspect of yourself.

The swords are as if struck by lightning. They radiate the vivid colours that stream from the woman.

DIVINATORY MEANING

If the message revealed in The Seven of Swords, that of creating distinct boundaries, is ignored, an eruption of anger can take place which needs to be safely released. The Eight of Swords indicates the need to free yourself of oppressive situations in order to re-create a happier and more purposeful life.

This card indicates a recognition of inner struggle, which leads to a process of 'letting go' in order to reach a solution. A sense of empowerment is created through channelling your emotions constructively.

9 OF SWORDS
MOURNING

THE IMAGE
It is night-time on Chalice Hill. In the sky, the moon is waning, and casts little light over the landscape. In the foreground a young man sits on his knees with his head in his hands. His skin is silvery-blue in the moonlight, and his tension is evident in the sharply defined muscles on his shoulders and back. His trousers are purple, the colour of mourning, and of spiritual insight, and this colour is reflected in the band that holds his long black hair back from his face.

Around him, nine swords form a semi-circle in order to help him contain his grief within safe limits. There is an opening at the front, and light shines from the figure and flows outwards. This signifies the need to allow yourself to feel grief and difficult emotions, so that they are not turned inwards to create illness. In being able to express your deepest feelings, they are fully released, as in The Eight of Swords. This creates a space within yourself for healing to take place, and once the emotion is spent, there is a feeling of relief, and an opening into new energy and opportunities.

DIVINATORY MEANING
It is necessary that you now allow yourself to grieve for what has been lost in the past. Through this, healing can be facilitated. It is important that you remember not to bottle-up your emotions, and that you allow yourself to receive any support that is offered to you.

No-one travels through life unscathed; emotional pain is one of the unpleasant facts of life. Yet it can also be seen as a gift, as long as it is recognised, and released, and not held on to. Mourning for what you have lost pierces your heart, and opens you up to new and deeper dimensions of feeling. The process brings about transformation through an expansion of awareness. The most sympathetic and empathetic people are those who have had the courage and strength to face, acknowledge, and release their own suffering.

10 OF SWORDS
REBIRTH

THE IMAGE

A man floats above the ground, gazing up at a mirror-image of himself that is suspended in the sky above him. Ten swords pierce the earth beside him, almost as if they are piercing his body. The man at the base of the image wears black trousers and a red shirt, signifying that he has come to terms with anger and pain, and is now ready to move away from it.

His mirror-image is a lighter version of himself. He is clothed in the blue of devotion, of inner calm and high spiritual ideals. They look at each other, each of them recognising that they are both aspects of the same person.

The figure close to the ground is aware that he has reached the lowest point in a cycle of his life. From here onwards the path leads upward, and he is resting awhile in order to regain his strength.

DIVINATORY MEANING

This card signifies the ending of a situation that has caused you much pain and sorrow. The grieving process represented in The Nine of Swords has now come to an end, and it is time to begin afresh.

Your experiences have taught you to connect in with, and relate to, the spiritual aspects of yourself. You now know that the material side of life has its importance and its pleasures, but is ultimately transitory. A quantum shift is taking place within you that promises to lead you to a new and more meaningful cycle in your life.

MAID OF SWORDS

THE IMAGE

A young woman holds a sword above her head, which glows red in the light of the dying sun. Her face is very determined, and warns you not to cross her path. Around her stand the ruins of the old church on top of Burrow Mump, Burrowbridge - a smaller version of Glastonbury Tor, dedicated, as the Tower on the Tor is, to St. Michael.

The Maid of Swords looks as if she is about to smash down the ruins. She is in a state of total rebellion against all confining structures and moral codes, and is bringing her great energy to bear in order to create change. Behind her, the archway opens out to reveal a beautiful, tranquil landscape, backed by hills, and divided by a river which reflects the colours of the sunset. This signifies the fresh beauty which can emerge once constraints have been released.

The green dress of the Maid shows that even in the midst of her desire for destruction of outmoded forms of behaviour, there is an underlying compassion, and the desire to create anew from what has been removed. Her stance looks harsh, but it is based on love which sees things as they truly are, and wishes to change them for the better.

The Ten of Swords showed the ending of a difficult period in life. The Maid has the courage to remove the final obstacles that block the way to a feeling of rebirth.

DIVINATORY MEANING

The Maid of Swords shows that it is time to rebel against any constraints that are holding you back or blocking your way. You are now realising what energy or people are keeping you from achieving your goal, and are ready to speak your mind, make your truth known, and change the situation.

This card shows a refusal to live up to unreasonable expectations imposed on you by others. You are now poised to create what you truly want in your life, with no fears or worries about how others will react to you. It is time to be uncompromising, to be willing to stand alone if you need to. In doing so, much will be accomplished.

KNIGHT OF SWORDS

THE IMAGE

The young Knight of Swords holds his glowing sword aloft, as he aims it to cut away the dead bramble branches at the bottom of Chalice Hill. Above him, on the rise of the hill, is the Lime tree depicted in The Moon card, and a grove of Ash trees. The presence of the lime tree shows that he is relying on his instincts and intuition to follow the course that feels right for him.

The Knight is clad in silver armour. He feels the need to protect himself from past hurts, and now takes the attitude of attack rather than defence in order to overcome obstacles. His face is determined, and the speed with which he is moving sends his hair flying across his face - signifying that it is necessary to look at the truth behind a situation before you act.

DIVINATORY MEANING

The Knight of Swords indicates a need to cut away the dead wood in your life. As with The Maid of Swords, a clearing process is taking place. Where The Maid of Swords is in a state of rebellion, The Knight has a definite purpose which entails a time of pruning, and of honing issues down into essentials.

This cards advises you to look at what is no longer needed in your life. If something no longer serves a useful purpose, it is time to let it go. New growth can take place once previous, unhelpful issues have been dealt with and released from your life.

QUEEN OF SWORDS

THE IMAGE

The Queen of Swords sits on a wooden throne before the roots of a tree on the Somerset Levels. Her throne is decorated very simply with golden diamond shapes that are reflected in the pattern of her green dress. At the top of the throne is a sun, surrounded by rays of light, signifying her ability to see clearly. The silken cloth that covers the seat of the throne is also golden-yellow, indicating that her mental powers are tuned to a high degree.

The Queen wears a blue velvet cloak, drawn closely around her body. Her search is for truth in its highest form; she expresses the deep devotion to truth that seers across the ages have spoken of, and she will stop at nothing in order to discover it. Her green dress, just visible beneath her cloak, indicates that she has compassion - but others may not find this immediately apparent, as she refuses any attempts at compromise.

Her sword is firmly held, pointing downwards, its sharp blade honed to a fine point. The hilt is tipped by a giant quartz crystal, signifying her clear-sightedness, and her ability to contact her vast inner power.

Beside her, lying on the grass, are two silver-grey masks which she has cut away from people who tried to deceive her. She is a woman who has suffered much, and has reached inner peace through the dramatic action represented by the Maid and Knight of Swords. She expects honesty from those around her, and will not tolerate anything less.

DIVINATORY MEANING

The Queen of Swords indicates that you have experienced a great deal in your life, and have passed through the veils of disillusionment to reach a still, uncompromising aspect of yourself. You desire from other people the open-ness and honesty that you yourself offer, and do not suffer fools gladly.

It is time to remove any masks that cover your true insight into a situation. Ensure that no-one is trying to 'pull the wool over your eyes'. You are now able to think clearly, and can employ your ability to be objective. It is time to use this with honesty and compassion.

KING OF SWORDS

THE IMAGE

The King of Swords sits on a golden throne, topped by sharp sun-like rays which indicate his powerful and astute mental faculties. His chin is raised, so that he looks down at you from the lofty heights of his great insight and wisdom. His expression is stern, yet benevolent - he is someone whom you can trust, and who is able to give good advice.

The King's cloak is a deep purple, signifying knowledge, wisdom, and the integration of spiritual insights. His blue tunic shows devotion to a cause or ideal, and his green trousers indicate creative thinking, and compassion. His boots are brown, symbolising a connection with the earth, and his feet are firmly anchored on the ground. The landscape behind him is clear and uncluttered like his mind, and the line of trees shows that he is able to create firm boundaries that should not be overstepped.

His sword is held firmly in both hands - he has complete control over his mental faculties, and his life. Its tip rests on the ground between his feet, indicating that he is able to use his insights in a practical way.

DIVINATORY MEANING

The King of Swords indicates the ability to see clearly. Whereas The Queen of Swords cuts away the masks of illusion, The King of Swords is able to dissipate them purely by the use of his clear vision.

This card means that you are now able to see clearly, and act upon your decisions. Obstacles can be easily overcome, and success is assured. This is a time to work hard towards fulfilling your ambitions, and there is likely to be good advice offered from someone in authority. Your powers of observation are sharp, and you have a deep sense of inner authority and confidence. Ensure that you feel grounded and centred, check all of the information available to you, and you will be able to forge ahead and realise your goal.

ACE OF VESICAS

ACE OF VESICAS

The Ace of Vesicas design is the ground plan upon which Glastonbury Abbey was built. This geometric design represents the grounding of spiritual energy so that it can be manifested on a practical level. Many ancient churches and sacred sites and buildings, including Stonehenge, are based upon this geometry.

THE IMAGE

The Ace of Vesicas floats like a many-faceted globe, suspended in whirling golden light. The two interlocking circles at its centre are delineated in orange, the colour of great joy and abundance. Within them are two interlocking hexagons, symbolising unification of energies. The points within the sign are linked by rays of light, and follow a pattern used by Kabbalists in the Tree of Life.

The colours in the design are rich and earthy. The deep red signifies the iron within the soil and also our blood which nourishes us and sustains us. The dark green is the colour of wealth and abundance, and the lighter green signifies growth, creativity, compassion and healing on all levels.

The circle within which the central vesica shape rests is a light golden colour, and shimmers against the earthiness of the deeper colour-tones. It looks rather like a bubble, enclosing and protecting the inner design. The circle is a symbol of continuity and wholeness, and reminds us of the infinite, eternal nature that is our essence.

DIVINATORY MEANING

The Ace of Vesicas indicates the ability to be fully grounded and earthed in reality. It signifies a state of balance and harmony, and reminds us that it is spirit which gives shape to all form.

This card shows a marked improvement in your financial situation, as it represents wealth on all levels of your life - material, emotional and spiritual. In a relationship, The Ace of Vesicas reveals that, as in all aspects of your life, there is a firm grounding that can be built upon.

2 OF VESICAS
CHANGE

THE IMAGE
A man wearing a kilt and beret whirls around as he throws two vesicas into the air at the pond in the grounds of Glastonbury Abbey. The sun shines on his back, marking out the areas of light and shadow, and reminding us that both are necessary to make us a whole person. His kilt and beret are shades of yellow and brown - he is grounded in the knowledge that there will always be high and low points in our lives, and both help us to understand and appreciate the other. His feet are bare - he feels his connection with the earth, and intends to maintain it.

One of the vesicas is flying upwards into the air, while the other is returning to the earth. The man is not attempting to catch or control their movement; he is unconcerned about outcomes because he is aware that all is as it should be, and is prepared to wait and see what happens. The surface of the lake is calm, disturbed only by gentle ripples.

DIVINATORY MEANING
The Two of Vesicas indicates that all life is based upon change. Nothing can remain static, and even endings lead into new beginnings. It is important at this time to go with the flow, and not attempt to manipulate events or situations. All things will come to you in due course.

This card suggests a change for the better, if you can be patient. It reveals an integration of the solar and lunar aspects of yourself, the powers of reasoning going hand in hand with the powers of intuition. The Ace of Vesicas has provided the necessary groundwork for the right energies to be attracted to you.

3 OF VESICAS
CREATIVITY

3 OF VESICAS
CREATIVITY

THE IMAGE

A man sits on a tree trunk, holding three vesicas in a pyramid shape. His legs are tucked beneath him, and rest against a plank of wood that partly covers a stone water container. Bales of straw rest under the tarpaulin behind him, ready for use in winter. A stone wall, representing clear boundaries, only partially hides the lush green landscape around the village of Compton Dundon.

The man wears a deep green sweater, symbolising creative energy, and the abundance that comes from focused hard work. His trousers are black, indicating that his energy is firmly grounded, and he loves his work and takes it seriously.

The pyramid shape that the vesicas are held in represents the ability to manifest ideas into actual form - much as a house was once an idea in the mind of an architect which then was drawn onto paper, and built by a builder.

DIVINATORY MEANING

The Three of Vesicas indicates rewards for hard work. This is a period of growth and steady progress. The expansion of your abilities and ideas leads to success because you are prepared to put effort into what you are doing.

This leads to recognition from others, and a sense of accomplishment.

4 OF VESICAS
INTEGRITY

THE IMAGE

A woman sits on a square seat covered in gold cloth in the grounds of Glastonbury Abbey. Behind her, the ruined walls are partly-covered in ivy, and the trees cast shadows in the sunlight.

The woman's bearing is erect. Her hands rest on her knees, adding to the aura of strength that emanates from her. She looks directly at you, and her face is calm and composed.

Her dress is the deep purple that denotes wisdom, and teaching abilities. Four vesica shapes glow; one at her solar plexus area, indicating that her will is strong; one in the heart area, signifying the ability to feel deeply, and to act on her feelings; and two on her shoulders, symbolising her ability and willingness to take on responsibility for her actions.

DIVINATORY MEANING

The Four of Vesicas indicates the need to deal with power in a constructive way. There is stability, and deep integrity in your dealings with others. You expect people to be as you are yourself, and are disappointed if they let you down. Either there is a need for more boundaries, or you are putting up too many barriers between yourself and others.

The Three of Vesicas showed the creative aspects emerging strongly. In The Four of Vesicas, this indicates providing the framework from which the fruits of creative thinking can emerge.

5 OF VESICAS
ENDURANCE

THE IMAGE

A figure sits huddled by a fire in a cave, once the hermit's cave on the slopes of Glastonbury Tor. The person could be male or female, and is wrapped tightly in a blue cloak to keep out the cold. The shade of blue indicates a search for spiritual truth, and the fire provides inspiration as well as warmth.

Outside, snow falls heavily on the slopes of Chalice Hill. It is midwinter, the sky is black, and five vesicas shine like stars. The image signifies a time of waiting, of cultivating patience despite difficulties, in the knowledge that eventually the weather will ease, spring will return, and new life will once more be apparent.

In the meantime, the figure sits, and waits, using this fallow time to dream, think, and make plans.

DIVINATORY MEANING

You are undergoing a testing time when you are occupied with issues that are very important to you. This brings with it an inner strength and fortitude that gives you the power to overcome problems.

This is a time when you can do little but wait, and make plans - the solution will present itself to you when you are in a clear frame of mind, and have set aside your anxieties. What is needed is for you to tend the fires of your imagination, and know that change is coming.

The integrity symbolised by The Four of Vesicas has to be tested in order to know itself fully. The uncomfortable situation depicted in The Five of Vesicas is about to shift towards the bright energy of Manifestation in the Six, the next card in this cycle. This knowledge can be used to comfort as well as spur you on. This card is like an initiation process, and will lead you to deeper self-knowledge.

6 OF VESICAS
MANIFESTATION

6 OF VESICAS
MANIFESTATION

THE IMAGE

This flower-like geometric pattern is actually a crop circle that appeared near Shepton Mallet, Somerset, just before Summer Solstice, 1998. Six vesica symbols are hidden within it, and six petals are shown in a double pattern, with a Star of David at its centre.

I have a strange, personal story to tell about this crop circle. The night that it appeared, I was driving home to Glastonbury from Shepton Mallet with a friend, when a huge, cerise-pink globe circled around and above the car, and followed us all the way to Glastonbury, disappearing behind the Tor. A large number of helicopters went that way minutes later, to investigate. The most remarkable part of this experience was that at one point, in the field where the crop circle was discovered the next day, the globe of pink light bounced like a huge yo-yo all over the field - then proceeded to resume tracking us!

When we heard the news of the crop circle the next day, we went to see it, and told a few people about the experience. We were informed that a sighting like this is quite common at the formation of crop circles. I found it interesting that the light we saw was pink, the colour of unconditional love, and the number of vesicas and petals in it was six - the number of The Lovers in the tarot. It is still a mystery. But it seemed an ideal image for this card - a manifestation of something unusual and beautiful.

DIVINATORY MEANING

The Six of Vesicas brings a feeling of great expansion that comes after a testing time. There is a huge influx of positive energy, and you are now able to reap the rewards of patience and hard work. There is a feeling of optimism, and you feel in tune with your heart energy, and are willing and able to give a great deal of yourself.

Something new is about to enter your life. A dream may be about to be realised, and it is a good time to think about what you really wish for in your life, and how you can bring it to fruition.

7 OF VESICAS
HARVEST

7 OF VESICAS
HARVEST

THE IMAGE

Through an archway in the grounds of Glastonbury Abbey, a woman carries a basket of fruit and vegetables. Behind her, flowers bloom in the arch of green, and the sun casts bright areas across the grass. Seven vesicas follow the curve of the archway, looking like glowing fruit.

The woman wears a radiant smile. Her purple top indicates that she has realised much, and has integrated her spiritual energy with her ability to be practical; she believes strongly in what she does, and her integrity shines through her. Her skirt is orange, the colour of joy and abundance.

The fruit and vegetables that the woman carries shine with health. They will nourish her mind as well as her body; she has grown them herself, and delights in their harvest and the rich reward it brings.

This card shows the ability to celebrate the gifts of life that were hinted at in the Six of Vesicas.

DIVINATORY MEANING

You have worked hard and willingly, with a sense of purpose. Now is the time to bring in the harvest, celebrate, and relax. There is a sense of accomplishment and achievement, and the knowledge that the rewards you are now about to reap will nourish you in every aspect of your life.

8 OF VESICAS
PATIENCE

8 OF VESICAS
PATIENCE

THE IMAGE

A craftsman sits on a chair, whittling a piece of wood. Small flakes of wood fall to the ground at his feet. Beside him are large figures that he has sculpted, and more rest on ledges on the white wall behind him that is set with vesica symbols also carved by him.

The white wall signifies that there is a purity in his work. It is simple, yet beautiful and unusual. The wood of the carved figures shines with a golden glow. He loves his work, and takes pride in it. The man's sweater is green, the colour of creativity, and his trousers are a deep blue, indicating that he is reliable and hardworking. His leather shoes bear the same sheen as his sculptures, showing that he cares for himself.

After the celebration and relaxation that comes from bringing in the Harvest of The Seven of Vesicas, it is time to begin again with renewed vigour.

DIVINATORY MEANING

You are able to use your creative energy to accomplish something that will be appreciated by others. It is important not to try to rush things in this process; you need to be prepared to allow things to take shape and come to fruition in their own time.

There is a feeling of inspiration and private happiness which flows through all that you do. Know that what you are working at now will bring its own rewards in the future, along with an inner sense of achievement.

9 OF VESICAS
GROWTH

9 OF VESICAS
GROWTH

THE IMAGE

A pregnant woman stands in her garden watering blossoming sunflowers with vesicas at their centres, which have not yet reached their full height. Behind her is a mass of violet flowers, and the sky hints at wide open spaces and is very blue.

The woman's dress is bright orange, the colour of hope and positivity. It flows over her body, revealing that she is close to giving birth to the baby she has yearned for. Her face is serene and happy; she knows that she has not long to wait until she will meet her child face to face.

In her hands she holds a large red and orange watering-can. Its colours represent happiness, and life-energy. The water it contains, and which she is sprinkling so carefully over the sunflowers is the stuff of life itself.

DIVINATORY MEANING

This is a time for tending the gifts that life has given you, and for giving thanks for what you have. In many tribal cultures, people give thanks to the universe before they receive its gifts, in the trust that all they hope for will be given to them.

In The Eight of Vesicas, the craftsman in the image felt a deep sense of satisfaction in his work. In The Nine of Vesicas, this feeling has developed into a sense of blessedness, of deep gratitude.

The Nine of Vesicas indicates a feeling of connection with the earth that so generously nourishes us. It also signifies fertility - though this can be of the body, or of the mind. A time of fruition is drawing near, and you can aid this by nurturing what is blossoming in your life.

10 OF VESICAS
WEALTH

10 OF VESICAS
WEALTH

THE IMAGE

In the grounds of Glastonbury Abbey, a blonde-haired woman holds a cornucopia containing three ears of corn, representing nourishment and celebration. As she tips the cornucopia, ten vesicas spill out like coins onto the grass.

Behind her, in the walls of the abbey, a doorway can be seen - a gateway into a new and beautiful life. Flowers border the path that leads towards it, and ancient trees lean over it as if to mark its entrance.

The woman wears a blue dress, symbolising the devotion she gives to everything she does. She is smiling happily, and her skin is radiant in the sunshine.

DIVINATORY MEANING

The Ten of Vesicas indicates abundance and wealth on all levels of your life - material, emotional, and spiritual. The promise of growth and new birth of The Nine of Vesicas has been fulfilled. There is a deep sense of appreciation, and a desire to share your good fortune with others.

With this card comes the awareness that "as you give, so shall you receive". Wealth is only a positive asset if you use what you have, and share it - otherwise it causes a feeling of miserliness and worry that it will be taken from you.

Your goals are being realised, and you feel fulfilled and at peace with the world.

MAID OF VESICAS

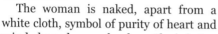

THE IMAGE

A beautiful pregnant woman, on the brink of giving birth, sits holding a vesica in the orchard near Chalice Hill. Behind the orchard, the Tor can be seen. It is late afternoon, and the sky is filled with the golden light so beloved in Glastonbury in the summer.

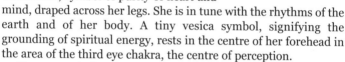

MAID OF VESICAS

The woman is naked, apart from a white cloth, symbol of purity of heart and mind, draped across her legs. She is in tune with the rhythms of the earth and of her body. A tiny vesica symbol, signifying the grounding of spiritual energy, rests in the centre of her forehead in the area of the third eye chakra, the centre of perception.

The woman's face is tranquil. She gazes down at a stream of golden energy that flows from her into the earth. Around her is a vibrant glow of pink shades, the colour of unconditional love, radiating outwards to golden tones that merge with the subtle light from the sky.

DIVINATORY MEANING

The Maid of Vesicas indicates a deep connection with the earth. Abilities can be developed in meditation and contemplation. This is a time of birthing new ideas and energy. It can mean motherhood, or the emergence of a new way of thinking.

This card is also connected with study - especially higher education, or psychology, or spiritual studies - as there is a deep curiosity about the world in which we live. It is a time of renewal, when all things seem fresh and inspiring.

KNIGHT OF VESICAS

THE IMAGE

A young man sits cross-legged on the ground on the outskirts of Glastonbury. His long black hair flows down his back, and his face is open and honest, with a hint of a smile.

He wears a deep red tunic, signifying mastery over the material aspects of himself. His trousers are orange, denoting positivity and energy. His hands are spread open, and his whole body glows with light.

KNIGHT OF VESICAS

Rising before him is a glowing vesica. He is using his willpower, awareness and control over matter to move it, and he is so in control of his energy that he does not even need to watch the vesica as it rises.

Behind him, some coppiced willow trees, a symbol of healing energy, are silhouetted against the light blue sky.

DIVINATORY MEANING

The Knight of Vesicas signifies mastery over the material aspects of life. It represents the ability to manifest what is needed in your life, through control of the will.

This card indicates thoughtfulness and compassion towards others, and a deep understanding that stems from inner knowledge gained through exploration of all aspects of the Self. You are able to tap into and rely on your own inner strength, because it has carried you through many experiences.

QUEEN OF VESICAS

QUEEN OF VESICAS

THE IMAGE

The Queen of Vesicas sits on a rock at the top of Ebbor Gorge, holding a vesica in her hand as if it were a shield. Behind her are the high cliffs and rocky terrain that she has just climbed, and in the distance the Tor with its tower is barely identifiable among the hills. The ground at her feet is bare and rocky, and stones in it glow in the soft sunlight.

The Queen wears a green dress, signifying compassion and healing. Around her head is a circlet of ivy, a plant that is able to survive against all odds, and literally clings to life.

Her face bears a half-smile, and also reveals that she is a strong woman who knows her own mind and will not suffer fools gladly. She is resting after the long and arduous journey, and the rock that she is seated on maintains her powerful connection with the earth.

DIVINATORY MEANING

The Queen of Vesicas indicates the overcoming of past obstacles and difficulties. You are grounded and centred within yourself, which gives you a sense of wholeness. This card indicates the need to be uncompromising about your goals and needs, but also to be able to see the humour in situations.

The Queen of Vesicas is able to draw upon the ability to manifest needs which was embodied by The Knight of Vesicas. You are a straightforward, honest person, able to take pleasure in what is going on around you, and your unerring sense of what is right for you will lead you to your goal.

There is the ability to go with the flow, and not try to push events before they are ready. This patience ensures the necessary preparation needed to fulfil your aims.

KING OF VESICAS

THE IMAGE

The King of Vesicas stands before a cliff-face covered in greenery at the entrance to Ebbor Gorge. Winter trees spread branches to the sky that look like roots, indicating the firmly grounded connection the King feels to the earth, and the material level.

The King gazes straight at you. His long hair is graying, and the light around his head reveals the wisdom of experience that he can offer to you. His face is kind, and looks as though he has experienced many cares in the past.

His cloak is the deep purple of wisdom and self-knowledge. It is fastened by an opal brooch, a stone that is hidden deep within the earth and has to be cracked open before its beauty can be seen by all. Beneath it, a vesica glows against his blue tunic.

DIVINATORY MEANING

The King of Vesicas signifies the ability to work hard in order to manifest desires. This card shows the need for form and structure in your life. It can indicate a businessman, lawyer, doctor, or someone in a position of authority.

You are on the brink of success, and will be able to enjoy the fruits and trappings of that success. The Queen of Vesicas showed that obstacles could be overcome. With The King, there is a state of inner peace that comes through confidence in your ability to accomplish what you set out to do.

BIBLIOGRAPHY

Ashe, Geoffrey *Mythology of the British Isles*. Methuen 1990

Ashe, Geoffrey *King Arthur's Avalon*. Collins 1957

Ashdown, Paul *Dunstan: Handbook for the Millennium*. Ashdown 1987

Baring-Gould, S *The Holy Grail*. Gothic Image 1977

Benham, Patrick *The Avalonians*. Gothic Image 1993

Caine, Mary *The Glastonbury Giants*. Mary Caine 1978

Caine, Mary *The Glastonbury Zodiac*. Grael Communications 1978

Caldecott, Moyra *The Green Lady & the King of Shadows*. Gothic Image 1989

Cavendish, Richard *King Arthur & the Grail*. Granada 1980

Coleman-Smith, Pamela and Waite, A.E. *The Rider-Waite Tarot*. US Games Inc.

Cunningham, Scott *The Encyclopaedia of Magical Herbs*. Llewellyn 1985, 1994

Cunningham, Scott *Crystal, Gem & Metal Magic*. Llewellyn 1991

Fryer, Jonathon and Craig, Chris *A Circle round the Sun: Journeys within the Glastonbury Zodiac*. Unique Publications, Glastonbury

Gibbs, Ray *The Legendary XII Hides of Glastonbury*. Llanerch 1988

Howard-Gordon, Frances *Glastonbury: Maker of Myths*, Gothic Image 1982, 1997

James, David, and Bostock, Simant *Celtic Connections*. Blandford 1996

Jones, Gwyn, and Jones, Thomas *The Mabinogion*. Dent 1949, 1975

Jung, Emma, and von Franz, Marie *The Grail Legend*. Coventure 1986

Lonegren, Sig *Labyrinths: Ancient Myths & Modern Uses*. Gothic Image 1991, 1996

Mann, Nick *Glastonbury Tor*. Annenterprise 1986

Mann, Nick *The Red & White Springs*. Triskele 1992

Matthews, John *A Glastonbury Reader*. Aquarian Press 1991

Matthews, John *The Mystic Grail*. Thorsons 1997

Matthews, John *Within the Hollow Hills*. Floris Books 1994

Matthews, John and Caitlin *The Arthurian Tarot*. Thorsons 1990

Michell, John *New Light on the Ancient Mystery of Glastonbury*. Gothic Image 1990

Moore, Robert, and Gillette D. *King, Warrior, Magician, Lover*. Harpercollins 1990

Order of the Rose Cross *The Legend of the Holy Grail*. London

Pollack, Rachel *Seventy Eight Degrees of Wisdom*. Thorsons 1997

Ryan, Mark, and Potter, Chesca *The Greenwood Tarot*. Harpercollins 1996

Smithett-Lewis, Lionel *Glastonbury & Her Saints*. Thorsons 1985

Treharne, R.F. *The Glastonbury Legends*. Abacus 1975

Williams, Professor Mary, *Glastonbury: A Study in Patterns*. RILKO

Williamson, Hugh Ross *The Flowering Hawthorn*. Peter Davies 1962

Zeigler, Gerd *Tarot, Mirror of the Soul*. Urania Verlags 1995